AGAP-OLOGY

Little Things I've Learned
About God's Big Love

by David Scherer

AGAPE★

Biblical quotations are from the New Revised Standard Version of the Bible,
© 1989, Division of Christian Education of the National Council of Churches of Christ
in the United States of America. Used by permission. All rights reserved.

All drawings by Dave Scherer
Cover photography by Stephen Holm
Cover and book design by Dan Miggler, Noiseland Industries
ISBN: 978-0-692-46559-2

Printed in the U.S.A.

Acknowledgements

Thank you to my wife for being my partner, counselor, editor, child-raiser, patience-provider, BS-detector, and soul-nurturer. You are the most beautiful human being I know.

Thanks to Bill Huff (Huff Publishing) and Susan Niemi for making sure that this thing got done.

Thanks to Andy Arnold, Dave Ellingson, Rich Mellheim, Steve Jerbi, Michael Bridges, George Baum, Heidi Hagstrom, and Jay Gamelin for being willing readers and strong theological minds.

Thanks to Luther and United Seminary professors Dwight Zscheile, Pat Kiefert, Kyle Roberts, Chris Scharen, Mary Jane Haemig, Michael Chan, Paul Chung, Guillermo Hansen, Mary Hess, Cameron Howard, Karoline Lewis, Alan Padgett, and Terry Fretheim. You all showed me that Christian orthodoxy is a wide stream and that there is actually a place for me within it.

Thanks to John Scherer, Dietrich Bonhoeffer, Tupac Shakur, Paul Tillich, Reinhold Niebuhr, Oscar Romero, Kendrick Lamar, KRS-One, Martin Luther King Jr., Rob Bell, Shane Claiborne, Nadia Bolz-Weber, Sara Miles, Anne Lamott, Rachel Kurtz, Lost And Found, Derek Webb, Fred Hammond, Karl Barth, James Cone, Michelle Alexander, Cornel West, Michael Eric Dyson, Howard Thurman, Emily Townes, Andy Root, and many others who I have "borrowed" from.

Thank you to the Scherer family for providing grist for the mill.

Thank you to Grandma Boone for being open to the Spirit. Thank you Mom for showing me that God's love gets bigger, never smaller. Thank you Stephanie for teaching me strength and celebration amidst difficulty. Thank you Jason Reed for introducing me to Hatija and having the courage to go to Bosnia. Thank you Pastor Kelly for taking a chance on me and showing me the vastness of God's *agape* love. Thank you to Blake for giving me my "biscuit." Thank you to Mikka for allowing me to experience the incredible place that is Haiti.

To all of you who have supported me over the years in my ministry,

THANK YOU!

CONTENTS

AGAP-OLOGY
Little Things I've Learned About God's Big Love

Introduction

In college I remember seeing a series of photos that ran in the *New York Times*. The first photo showed an angry mob of college students chasing a white supremacist down the street. You can tell from the photo that the mob is not looking to have a constructive peace-making dialogue when they catch him. In the second photo the crowd is beating the neo-Nazi with their sticks and fists. It's the left side of the second frame that still trips me out to this day. In it you see an eighteen-year-old African American woman who has draped her body over the man . . . to protect him. You can see a look of desperation on her face as she pleads with the crowd to stop. If the mob was going to keep punching him, they were going to also have to punch her. At the bottom of the frame you see the skinhead looking at the woman's lifesaving gesture as if he was looking at a unicorn.

I consider myself to be a pretty nice dude. But the idea of jumping on top of a Nazi to save his life from a crowd of angry people has never crossed my mind. This kind of crazy enemy love is called "agape" in the Greek language. This love isn't "OMG, I *love* Kim Kardashian's new purse." *Agape* is God's redemptive goodwill for all of humankind.

The writer of John 3:16 says, "God so loved the *world*" ("loved" is *agape* in Greek). The writer didn't say:
"God so loved the people that agree with me."
"God so loved the people that make me feel comfortable."
"God so loved the people that don't bug the crap out of me."
Shoot the verse doesn't even say:
"God so loved the people who aren't complete A-holes."

A better translation in English is actually "God so loved the *cosmos*." This means that God loves the WHOLE FREAKING UNIVERSE!

I was introduced to the concept of *agape* in college when I read a sermon from Martin Luther King Jr. He said, "An overflowing love which seeks nothing in return, *agape* is the love of God operating in

I

the human heart." I chose AGAPE* as my stage name and have tried to "AGAPE*" the world with this love ever since. I have considered it a privilege to get to know the stories of so many people from so many different walks of life and listen for God at work. These stories have become a big part of my ministry. People have often said to me something like, "Hey, your music is okay but I was wondering if you have any of your stories written down anywhere." (Translation: "Your music sucks but I might like your stories.") I decided that I would try to write down some of these stories in hopes that they might help someone. It's a little audacious for me to write a book (but it's also audacious to call yourself "God's love" so why stop now?). I am not a pastor. I am not a writer. I am not a trained theologian. I am just a dude. But my hunch is that God might use one of these stories to give a "biscuit" to someone who needs it.

Some people might use this book for their personal devotional time. Maybe some youth directors might play my CD and use these stories with their students. But you know what would really make my day? I would love it if the sewing ladies in church basements would read this book and listen to my CD while they made someone a quilt!

You have permission to write in this book. There is a "write/draw" section in each chapter where you can write, draw, journal, and so forth. Take advantage of it. You can disagree with this book (email me at info@hiphopoutreach.com). You can give it away and ask for more (if we have extra copies and are feeling generous we might hook you up with another one ☺). You can do the recommended action steps at the end of each chapter or come up with your own. You can even draw crazy pictures like I did. As long as you think about God's *agape* love in your life. Throughout my ministry I feel like people probably see me perform and say, "He's not even that good. I could rap better than that!" That's been the point. I have always hoped that my music would inspire others to share their song. This book is no different. My feeble attempt at writing these stories is a way of saying to everyone, "Your story matters. So tell it!" When we share our stories (especially with those who are different from us), we develop more compassion for each other. This is exactly what we need right now.

I am currently watching the results of human hatred on the news and feel even more convicted about the urgency of our situation. The world is groaning for liberation that only *agape* love can provide. This love is bigger than our fears. This love is bigger than our doubt. This love continues to pursue us whether we deserve it or not. *Agape* love is the healing, mercy, joy, redemption, presence, forgiveness, solidarity, welcome, patience, reconciliation, grace, and justice of our God. So pursue it. Receive it. Learn it. And share it. The suffix "-ology" comes from the word *logos*, which means "word." So "AGAP-OLOGY" is basically "words" of "love" from me to you. Enjoy! Shalom.

Think
Think about the ways that you have seen *agape* love show up in your life. Reflect on how you can share that love with others.

Talk
1. When you hear the word *love*, what is the first word that pops up in your mind (don't think about it for a long time and don't filter your thoughts)?
2. Talk about a time when you experienced God's *agape* love.
3. Describe a situation in which you would be willing to lay down your life to save someone else's life. Would you do this for an enemy? Why or why not?
4. How do you try to share God's *agape* love with the world?

Act

Think about a way to love someone who has really annoyed you throughout your life. Pray that God would give you strength.

Pray

Dear God, thank you that you love the whole world enough to pour yourself out for each one of us. Show us how to love those who are difficult to love. Fill our hearts with agape love so that the world might know how much you care about them. In your name we pray, Amen.

Write/Draw

"Agape Love" by AGAPE*
Featured on *Enough*

A is for the Africans chilling in the cut.
E is for the Europeans. What! What!
GAP that's the gap.
I'd rather bust a prayer than bust a cap.
There's different types of love that we got for each other.
Philos that's the love I got for my brother.
Eros that's the love I got for my girl.
Agape that's for everybody in the world.
Check it, hate is what we're caught in.
Heaven's what we're not it.
God so loved the world that He gave his only begotten
to show us how to love right
black white keep it tight every night
'cause inside of us there is a light.
Down like that clown around like that.
The color doesn't matter red, brown, white, black.
A sound like that must be from God above.
Not Eros, not philos, but Agape love.

CHORUS:
We're all equal nobody's above.
Let's stop that hate and spread that love (Agape Love) (2x)

Mic jack white black like that tight track
coming up, yo the devil wanna fight back.
AGA to PE VL to GD
we spread love just like graffiti.
Why we spreading hate? Getting late for that.
Hate eliminates it'll break your back
shake the track love heals love's real.
Hating strangers bringing danger like a drug deal.
Thugs feel pain they cry in the rain.
We got the same things that we're trying to attain.
Whether flying a plane amidst the doubt.
Or walking on the sand to see what it's about.
Twist and shout when you find your savior and He's with you.
Then you realize that he never did forget you (it's agape love)

(CHORUS)

Will you forgive me for the times that I messed you up?
Will you forgive me for the times I oppressed you up?
Dressed you up in a robe of judgment. (That's my bad)
We're family I realize your dad is my dad.
I had prejudice in me but I don't know
how it got there I tell it to leave but it won't go.
I try to love you as much as He loves us
Agape over eros love above lust
a dove crushed everytime we're spreading the hate
love agenda got lost now we're setting it straight.
I'm coming up on the love and can't nothing hang.
God shot His love into me with a sudden bang.
Wasn't a thang to love you a little more.
You tell me Matthew 5:44
"Love your enemies and pray for those who persecute you"
that's even your foes.
Agape trying to get 12 hugs a day.
What I need to do yall is Agape.

(CHORUS)

I love you just because God made you and He made me.
I love you black white gentleman and lady.
I love you bird. I love you moon. I love you trees.
I love you sun. I love you rain. I love you breeze.
I love you black man.
I love you member of the Ku Klux Klan, Iraq and Iran.
I love you Christian. I love you Muslim.
I love you Mecca. I'm loving you Jerusalem.
I love you straight. I love you gay.
That's the love of God (help me) Agape.

NOTE: This song and all the others in the book are available on iTunes.

Chapter 1

Diamond Ring
The Redemption of AGAPE*

*For I am convinced that neither death, nor life, nor angels, nor rulers,
nor things present, nor things to come, nor powers, nor height, nor depth,
nor anything else in all creation, will be able to separate us from the love
of God in Christ Jesus our Lord.* Romans 8:38–39

There's a Leonard Cohen song that says, "It's the cracks that let the light in." I think eighth grade was the year I started figuring out what the heck my brother Leonard was talking about. That was the year that my Grandma's fifty years of puffing on unfiltered Chesterfields finally caught up to her. Lung cancer shouldn't have felt so surprising to us. I guess I never thought prim southern women were susceptible to such a messy disease, but cancer is a heartless beast. "Stage 4 terminal lung cancer" has the potential to cause dignified demure women to fade into undignified pale skeletons while their family has to sit by and watch helplessly. I was worried that my Grandma Boone, the orderly southern belle, was about to be tossed around wildly by the uncontrollable mutation of uncooperative cells. It wasn't fair. I was scared for her . . . and for me. I forgot about the possibility that the "crack" of cancer was going to be what we needed for the light to enter into our lives. Sometimes it is precisely the sickness that brings the healing.

Healing was exactly what my grandma's spirit needed. She had spent many of her years married to my alcoholic grandfather until they finally divorced. She got sick of him pawning all of her jewelry to get money for whiskey. Who she really had wanted to marry was this French count named "Gerard." Gerard (he just sounds handsome doesn't he?) was a French student she had fallen in love with while she was studying in Paris at the Sorbonne University. With a glimmer in her eye, she confessed to my step mom before she died that Gerard was her first love. They were separated by the war and eventually married others. Just when we would want to hear more about Gerard and Grandma's days in France, the moment would be gone.

As my grandma was about to turn seventy-five, my step mom had a brilliant idea. The seventy-fifth birthday is considered a diamond birthday. The best way to symbolize this would be to get her a *diamond ring!* After all, jewelry had become a symbol for her painful marriage. My step mom and dad wanted to reclaim this for her. Why not give her the chance to finally wear a beautiful precious stone? This would complete the circle. They sat there for a moment, pondering the absurdity of making such a frivolous purchase for a woman who was dying. But when you're staring death in the face nothing seems all that crazy anymore. They took a trip down to the local pawnshop and found a perfect diamond perched on the top of a shiny gold band. On the morning of her birthday a dozen of us crammed into her tiny room and sang "Happy Birthday" as she playfully conducted. Then, a red velvet box was given to her that contained some of the finest "bling" in all of Spokane. She grinned from ear to ear as she slipped the ring easily onto her slender finger. For the next few weeks, we would wheel her around in public as she flashed her rock to anybody who was willing to look. "Check it out!" she would say proudly to her friends at church. She must have showed the whole city that ring. Score one point for the light, darkness zero. The "cracks" of cancer were doing their job.

Each day we would creep down the stairs to see if Grandma was still moving. Once we saw her shuffling bedsheets we would pump our fists in celebration. "Another day to live!" we would shout. She was cheating death, and we knew that we were playing with house money. Grandma would occasionally look at us and ask us with a deadpan delivery, "Am I dead yet?"

"No Grandma, you're not dead *yet*. We are so glad too, because we love you."

"I love you too," she would fire back casually, as if ignoring the fact that she had scarcely uttered those three words to any of us in her previous seventy-five years of being alive.

I never wanted to leave her room because I never knew what kind of sacred moments were going to pop up out of nowhere. Our day would weave seamlessly in and out of "Wheel of Fortune," pain prescriptions, and existential questions about the universe. We began to talk about death so matter-of-factly that I started to forget how scary a proposition it actually was. Discussions of the fate of human souls became as common as the weather for us. "I wonder if it will snow today. Oh, and Grandma, do you think your dad will be able to sing with you for eternity in heaven?" We read something called *Emmanuel's Book* that said, "Death is like taking off a tight shoe." Grandma clung to that phrase. It became her mantra as she prepared to pass on.

During those final days I would peer into the French doors of her room and see my grandma and my dad chatting away. They would lean in close and hold each other tenderly. My grandma would insist that she had blown it as a mom. My dad would hug her and repeat over and over, "You did well, Mom. You did well." After weeks of this daily ritual, the shame and guilt that my grandma was carrying began to slowly melt away. The ring, the birthday party, the conversations with her son—it was all mending her soul right before our eyes. But there was one more heart surgery that needed to be finished before she could be discharged. My step mom knew exactly what it was: "We need to get a hold of Gerard!"

We desperately searched through old numbers and then recruited a French-speaking friend to track him down as Grandma's condition worsened. The friend enlisted the help of French operators who were charmed by this love story and found Gerard's number. We knew we didn't have much time. My dad tried the number over and over with no luck. Before giving up, he called one last time. And then, the voice of an elderly man answered the phone in French, *"Bonjour."* It was Gerard!

Hopped up on morphine, drifting in and out of consciousness, and less aware of what was going on around her, Grandma heard my step mom come in the room and whisper to her, "Boone, Gerard is on the phone." Her eyes opened and she became fully present. "Gerard?" she asked, as her voice went up two octaves. Fixing her hair and smoothing out the wrinkles in her robe she took the phone from my dad. At this point she became less like a dying grandma and more like a woman in love. "Just tell him about your life for the last five decades," my dad said to her. "You guys should have plenty to catch up on." She moved the receiver slowly toward her ear in disbelief. They talked and talked a long time while trading stories about their lives and their wonderful memories together. We all sat and watched this moment as we cried beautiful tears.

As she let him go, she playfully blew a kiss into the phone and said, "*Au revoir,* Gerard." Shortly after her conversation with Gerard, she began to fade back into semi-consciousness again. Her breathing became more peaceful and less frequent. Her focus was deeply inward. And then, just a few days after her magical phone date, the sheets stopped moving. My grandma said her final *au revoir* while she took off her tight shoe. She was free.

How is it that Christ's love is still able to sneak up on us when we least expect it? I'm talking about when we are at our lowest low. Our hearts are surrounded by huge, hundred-foot, impenetrable walls, and somehow God's bulldozer finds a way to still show up and knock them down. Beginning in Romans 8:32, Paul gives this long list of things that cannot separate us from God's love. "Will hardship, or distress?" Paul asks rhetorically. He starts rattling them off, "neither death, nor life, nor angels, nor rulers, nor things present, nor things to come . . ." And then he finally concludes with "nor anything else in all creation" (v. 38). I believe that with this line Paul is giving us license to fill in the blank with our own hardship. "Not sadness, not addiction, not cancer, not divorce, not self-injury, not racism, not depression, not sexual assault, or homelessness." And it can keep going, "Not unemployment, not poverty, not low self-esteem, not greed, not violence, not abuse, not failure, not shame, and so forth."

Time and time again, I have seen God's love sneak in at the last minute to bring redemption to a situation that seemed hopeless. It would have been easy to write my grandmother off when she had lost her spark. Those last six months as she was dying was the first time that Grandma actually had a chance to live. Through the Spirit's work, my grandmother figured out that it is never too late to find happiness. It's never too late to reconcile with your son. It's never too late to call "old flames." And it's absolutely NEVER too late to buy a beautiful diamond ring. Rest In Peace Boone Young. Shalom.

Think
Think about a few of the most difficult circumstances that you have faced in your life. Now reflect on Paul's words that there is nothing that can separate us from God's love.

Talk
1. "It's the cracks that let the light in." Describe a time when you experienced this phenomenon.
2. Have you ever had someone close to you pass away? Did you see or feel God show up anywhere in the situation?
3. What would you do if you knew that you would die in less than a month? How would you live your life differently?
4. Do you believe in a literal resurrection of Jesus? Do you think *we* will also be resurrected? Explain.

Act
Choose one thing that you can do to live life more fully in response to all that God has done. Ask God to lead you and knock down the walls of fear that you have put up.

Pray

God of life, thank you for each moment that we have here on earth. Remind us that it is never too late to live out your love and forgiveness in our lives. As we reflect on those who have passed away, remind us of your promise that not even death can separate us from you. Amen.

Write/Draw

Make a "bucket list" of ten things that you want to do before you die (forgiving someone, having a unique experience, and so forth).

"Separate Us" by *AGAPE**
Featured on *Sprinkle Sunshine*

Picture a queen with a style that would light up the room.
Picture a scene where her smile was like a perfume.
She had a dream as a child that was right in the womb.
It didn't seem that somehow it was happening soon.
She wanna be a ballerina dance on the moon.
At 15 all her ballerina plans are doomed.
Her family serves low self esteem for breakfast.
She wears all her heart felt dreams for a necklace.
A pretty southern miss why she cut her wrist?
Her daddy wasn't there so she found men to hug and kiss.
She started clubbing with no rubbers had a couple kids.
She used to drop it like it's hot she needed oven mitts.
She discovered this love it was on another tip.
She felt unlovable unworthy and unequipped.
One trip to the altar with the flock stop and called to the rock
Of Gibraltar shocked 'em all a lot
Now she's involved with her walk and her calling is solid rock.
You can't stop this. You can't knock this.
All the walls in the world can't block this.
Nothing can separate her.
From the L.O.V.E. of the creator.

CHORUS:
Not death nor life
Can separate us from the love of Christ

In this next story where we start
Is the sad chapter of these high school sweethearts.
It was hard to be apart he and his brigade
Had a couple more missions then he'd come home and he'd get paid
Everyday she would choke tears back
She was so scared that he would die any day.
Anyway, sure enough she gotta call
2 year old baby there and she saw it all
"We regret to inform you that your husband is gone.
He served his country well and his legacy will live on"
She dropped the phone like the bombs that her husband was close to
She tried to calm her baby like a mother's supposed to.
All she wanted was one more kiss.
She prayed to God that it wouldn't have to end like this.
She heard 21 guns watched them fold the flag.

It wasn't real she hoped that he might come back.
They said, "your husband was the stallion of his battalion.
His effort was valiant." so they gave her a medallion
She didn't want that she wanted him back.
So with tears in her eyes and her daughter on her lap she cried.

(CHORUS)

Not famine not disease not war. (can hold ya back from Christ)
Not fear nor shame (can hold ya back from Christ)
Not crime not poverty not divorce (can hold ya back from Christ)

Not death not life not wrong nor right can hold ya back from Christ

Chapter 2

Big 'Ole Jesus
The Welcome of AGAPE*

In my Father's house there are many dwelling places. If it were not so, would I have told you that I go to prepare a place for you? And if I go and prepare a place for you, I will come again and will take you to myself, so that where I am, there you may be also. John 14:2–3

If there are a lot of rooms in our Father's house, then my family's dwelling place was way out on the porch somewhere. Theologically we were the equivalent of one of those crazy aunts who collects everything and hoards it. If there was an existing religious path, my family had tried it, chanted it, and bought the cassette tapes for it. This spiritual potpourri of memories fills up my senses as I reflect on my childhood.

First, there was the pulse in my chest from the banging drums as we ushered in the Pagan solstice. Then, there were the reverberating echoes in my ears of our family's Sanskrit chants ("ohhhhmmmm") at the dinner table. In my mouth I can still taste the bitter herbs and sweet apples from the Jewish Seder meal that we would participate in annually. In my nose is a mixture of *nag champa* and marinated tofu from our family's trips to the *ashram* in Pennsylvania. And how could I forget about my hands rubbing the smooth belly of the large wooden Buddha statue that was plopped in the middle of our living room. My parents wanted to expose me to as much beauty and wisdom as they could. They believed that the power of God's love was so big that it could not be contained in just one religion.

One day I was at a Christian Fellowship event at my college, and I was bragging about all of the interesting religious experiences that I was blessed to have growing up. A friend of mine named Lisa interrupted me, "Dave, this is not good. The devil uses these things as a tool to trick us. God has told me that you need to go home as soon as you can and witness to your mom. If you really love her this is the right thing to do."

I was jealous of Lisa's uncanny ability to always hear God's voice. Whether it was a deep matter of salvation or which burrito to order at Chipotle, she seemed to always have her laptop linked directly to God's router. Her concern for the destination of my mother's soul gave me pause. What if she was right? After all, my mom had never talked about a born-again experience with Jesus. What if she actually *was* going to burn for eternity? What if I had the chance to convert her and didn't do it? Would her torched soul be on my hands? That seemed kind of silly but I didn't want to risk it. And besides, I had experienced so much joy and freedom during my own Jesus transformation. Maybe my mom could use the same thing in her own life. I thought to myself, "I'm already scheduled to go home in a few days to do laundry. Maybe I can kill two birds. I'll wash my clothes and my mom's sins on the same trip." As I prepared to go home and "witness" to my mom, my brain was flooded with all sorts of soteriological questions:

What if she died before I got there to present the gospel to her?

What if my mom burned in hell for eternity because I didn't get back in time?

What if there are others in my life that might suffer the same fate?

These questions were keeping me up at night. I couldn't wait any longer. I went home a day early just to hedge my bets. As I made the hour-long drive back to Minneapolis, I started rehearsing the speech that I was going to give to my mom to "save her soul."

I was going to start out something like,

"Hey mom, I know you love me right?"

She did love me. More than any other human being I had ever met. The compassion, peace, joy, and hope that I had inside of me were all because of my mother. Hadn't I heard somewhere that "God is love"? If my mom is so full of love, doesn't that mean that she is full of God too?

Line two of the speech was,

"Mom, you have to say this prayer with me."

Wait, she has to speak words to get God to love her and accept her? Like it's a magic password or something? Is God really that petty? Is God like a genie that doesn't come out of the bottle until you say the right words? And, what about people who are mute and can't even say the right words or who have an IQ too low to understand the words they are saying?

Line three:

"God is not happy with who you are, Mom."

But why would God create someone and then hate that someone enough to send her to eternal punishment in fire? Isn't God supposed to be slow to anger and rich in love? I wouldn't even make my worst enemy drown in a pool of fire. And I'm not even that nice of a guy!! You have to think God is more gracious and compassionate than me, right?

Line four:

"Your spiritual path is not the right one."

But what about the time when Jesus told a Samaritan with leprosy and a Canaanite woman that their faith made them well even though they didn't have the "right" faith? What about all of the Holy Spirit activity that I witnessed growing up in our house where the word Jesus *wasn't even uttered? What about the two-thirds of the world that is on a different spiritual path than Christians? Is God too small or ineffective to be able to use other paths to reach people before they go to hell? Or does God secretly want them to burn in hell? That would be sadistic.*

The last line:

"You need to repent for your sin."

What gives me the qualifications to judge my mom like that? Was it my job to point out everyone else's sin? Doesn't Jesus say, "Let the person who doesn't ever screw up throw rocks at people"?

Given all my screw-ups, I decided I should probably keep all of my rocks in my own pocket. By the time I made it to home to Minneapolis, I had scrapped my speech to my mom. If God's house really has so many dwelling places then my mom was going to be fine. I had decided this: Love with an agenda isn't love. I was going to love my mom with my actions, not with my words. So that weekend I never spoke the word *Jesus* to my mother. Instead I preemptively cleaned her house. I cooked without being asked. I washed the dishes cleaner than they had ever been. She was blown away, "Whatever they are doing to you in college, I love it!" she exclaimed.

My life-changing encounter with Jesus has now allowed me to see God at work in many different places, including the *ashram* and the solstice drum celebration. Choosing to walk the Christian path has not made me *less* tolerant of other faiths, but has made me *more* aware of how God can show up in any old place if you're not careful. I long for my perspective of Jesus to become bigger not smaller. I long for a faith in Jesus that makes me *more* welcoming and accepting of others not *less* accepting. I imagine that God is preparing a dwelling place for my family where we get to be who God made us to be: solstice-dancing, Sanskrit-chanting, Seder meal-having, tofu-loving, Buddha-appreciating children of God that prefer the porch. My guess is that Jesus will come visit us out there to dance with us or have a glass of wine. And maybe we can even get Lisa to come out there every once and a while too! ;-) Shalom.

Think
Would you be disappointed if everyone made it to heaven? Reflect on this.

Talk
1. How do you think God feels toward those who do not self-identify as "Christian"?
2. How do you try to witness your faith to others who are not Jesus' followers?
3. Describe what you think "hell" is. What about heaven?
4. Has your journey with Jesus made you more welcoming and accepting of others or less so? Why?

Act

Learn about a faith that is different from yours. Seek out someone who comes from a different religious tradition and try to learn as much as you can. Look for ways that God is present in another tradition.

Pray

Dear God, thank you that your love is so big. You use people and traditions that are outside of our comfort zone to communicate your love to the world. Open our hearts to the bigness of your love so that we can engage with those from other faiths and love them the way that you do. Use us to shine a light and proclaim your love to the world in a way that is compassionate and open-minded. In your big love we pray, Amen.

Write/Draw

"Trust In Grace" by AGAPE*
Featured on *Paradoxology*

My God's garage has a lotta cars in it
Room for the Maserati and the dodge Plymouth
and the Honda civic with the tinted windows
Nobody knows which way the wind blows

CHORUS:
God will reconcile all creation we know it will be alright
Saints and sinners both gain salvation we can celebrate tonight
Trust in mercy. Trust in grace
Every nation tribe and race

You've been down since the days of girbauds
and the tags on our clothes
and the phases that were going around
Impressed and I'm blessed never would have guessed
When I moved west you still came to town
I'm grateful
You always came around like April
You say you've never been into God
Chances of going up to synagogue since Kindergarten's
less than Ahmadinejad (I won't push you)
Matter fact I'm figuring out my own issues
We've been best friends ever since the third grade
I fought 'em when they said you weren't saved
In my church they told me through some word play I should turn away
From my friend who'd spent with me every birthday since I turned eight
Who deserves grace in the first place?
Not us gotta trust in in the mercy (3x)
And that's the end of the verse (hey)

(CHORUS)

A son of Barbara sue that's who I am
We really weren't a church going fam
But I know you know the story of Jehova's glory
Sacrifice cut your stomach open for me
Loved me and adored me warmly ever since
six presidents I represented poorly
But you still showed Christ love
Didn't call it Christ love
You called it that bigger than life love

And that's what your life was
It's amazing what a little bit of light does
I was told that because you pray in a new way
That you're going to stay in H.E. blank blank cool j
Like Lupe waiting in the line you won't make it in time
And you're gonna need a toupee
Head scorched with pitchfork
Twisted morbid Christians wished for it
Trying to prove they were so right
They'd be mad if we all had eternal life

(CHORUS)

I'm counting on the trampoline
Bounce back when I fall now I'm redeemed
Bounce bounce back bounce back

Chapter 3

Drag Race
The Mercy of AGAPE*

*As a mother comforts her child, so will I comfort you;
you shall be comforted in Jerusalem.* Isaiah 66:13

Growing up, my mom was like Batman for me (except for the cape and funny-looking Underoos). I felt that her utility belt of love could save me from any difficult situation. But, let's be real, you don't want to mess with the Caped Crusader. She was a single mom who knew how to enforce justice on me when I was acting like a Joker. I was a pretty good kid for the most part. But sometimes Gotham City gets the best of you. Especially that one time when I had just gotten my driver's license . . .

I blame it all on my friend STEPHEN. STEPHEN was the Johnny Depp of Southwest High School (you always have to capitalize his name because he was that freaking cool). He flashed his devilish dimples and asked me to drag race through the crowded streets of Minneapolis at high speeds while narrowly avoiding death. Like a prepubescent wimp from a bad after-school special, I caved in to the cool kid. To be fair, STEPHEN was really, really cool! Did I mention how cool he was?

We began our drag race by revving our "hot rods" side by side. Mine was a 1985 silver Honda Civic hatchback. And STEPHEN? He had a non-ironic, barely street-legal, blue, 1987 Chrysler minivan. Praying to the ghost of Dale Earnhardt, we ran through stop signs at fast speeds as we vied for the title of "Hooptie Drag Race Champion." I whooshed past STEPHEN (albeit a slow whoosh) through the finish line as I pumped my fists in victory. Suddenly my celebration was interrupted by the sound of sirens. I quickly realized that these weren't coming from the N.W.A. song that was blasting from my stereo. These were the "real thing." A towering officer with a pristine, black uniform and a big old gun approached my car. After peeing on myself, I attempted to readjust my reclined "pimp seat" and turn down the abrasive music. I had heard that police don't tend to like over-swagged-out kids who listen to N.W.A. (those who know N.W.A.'s music know why). This officer was like an intimidating drill sergeant from a bad Maury Povich episode. "You're going to jail, son!" he shouted. "We are going to lock you up for reckless driving, running a stop sign, speeding, public endangerment, and rapping every word to 'Straight Outta Compton' (even though you actually live in Linden Hills)."

Meanwhile all I could think about was facing the Dark Knight at home. She was not going to be happy. After insulting me for a few minutes, the officer calmed down. "We're not going to throw you guys in jail," he said. "Instead we are going to tell your parents." Little did he know. Based on what would be waiting for me at home, jail was a much better option for me at that point.

I started to drive home to the bat cave as I contemplated my fate: *I wonder which method my mom is going to use to kill me . . . Shotgun? Rusty knife? Some torturous killing device that she keeps in her basement that no one has ever seen?*

I did my freaked-out tortoise mosey up to the WD-40-deprived back door. An inconspicuous entrance was not in the cards. I was dead meat. I practiced my excuse a few times ("see-what-had-happened-was-we-were-carjacked-by-a-gang-of-fairies-and-they-made-us-drag-race-with-each-other . . ."). Then I took a deep breath and made my way across the creaky wood floors. A very disturbing noise began to bellow from the upstairs. It sounded like a teenage-eating-fire-breathing dragon, but I was pretty sure that it was my mother. As she inched closer, I launched into an incoherent babbling plea, "see-what-had-happened-was-guys, um, cars, uh, fast, eh, boom, eek, police . . . please, mom, I'm too young to die."

"Come here," she said. Apparently she liked her victims to be close before she executed them. This was a smart move on her part. I gasped as she inched toward me and held out her arms. And then . . . she did something that still freaks me out to this day . . . SHE HUGGED ME!

She lifted me up into the sky in a passionate embrace as she squeezed all of the remaining air out of me. She wouldn't let go. "I'm so glad you are okay," she said kissing my forehead and twirling me around like a rag doll. "I didn't know where you and STEPHEN were. I was so worried about you two."

Once it finally registered what she was doing, I was utterly confused. Why was she not punishing me? I closed my eyes and let her cleansing hug wash over me. I was forgiven.

There was nothing I did to earn this forgiveness.

It was a gift she gave me simply because she loved me that much.

She didn't need my excuses.

Heck, she didn't even need an apology at that point.

All she cared about in that moment was that I had come home.

That was enough for her.

Her love for me was bigger than all of my screw-ups.

I couldn't talk my way out of this love.

I didn't talk my way into this love.

All I could do was just be present to it, accept it, and enjoy it as a free gift. That's when I figured it out: "God's love is like my mom's!"

Some people might be surprised (or even offended) to hear me talk about God's love being like a mother. But throughout our scriptures there are references to the feminine qualities of God. In the book of Proverbs, we encounter Lady Wisdom ("Chokmah"), the one who was with God "before the beginning of the earth" (Proverbs 8:23).

But it's in the book of Isaiah that I find my favorite image of God's mothering nurture. In this story, we see a people not living up to their potential of what they could be. You might say that Israel was in its reckless "drag racing" phase. They forgot who they were, in a sense. They neglected justice for the poor and vulnerable. They disobeyed God. They were wallowing in guilt, shame, and desperation, making up excuses for why they hadn't held up their end of the bargain. They were dead meat. They didn't want to face the music. Instead of a fire-breathing dragon waiting to kill them, they heard these words: "As a mother comforts her child, so will I comfort you" (Isaiah 66:13). Bam! Blindsided by grace like a big unexpected hug from out of nowhere. How liberating—and strange—it would have been for them to hear those compassionate words from God in that moment. The word for "compassion" in Hebrew is *rachamim,* a word that is related to the Hebrew word for "womb" (*rechem*). The one who birthed us is also the one who loves us like we are a part of her. Our Big Divine Momma wishes to gather us together "as a hen gathers her brood under her wings" (Matthew 23:37). Our loving "Ima" holds us in her lap, wipes our tears, and lets us know that everything is going to be okay. There is nothing we can do to earn this forgiveness. It is a gift she gives simply because she loves us that much. She doesn't need our excuses. Heck, she doesn't even need an apology. All she cares about is that we come home. That is enough for her. Her love for us is bigger than all of our screw-ups. We can't talk our way out of it. We can't talk our way into this love. All we can do is just be present to it, accept it, and enjoy it as a free gift.

In light of these experiences and divine feminine scriptures, I have started beginning my prayers from time to time with "Our Mother, who art in heaven." I think it has a ring to it. By the way, I still know STEPHEN. He's *still* the coolest kid in the room. And my mom continues to be cooler than Batman ☺. Shalom.

Think

Think about God as a mother waiting at home for you with a big hug. Picture the Holy Spirit as a mother eagle hovering over all of the darkness of your life. Her loving intentions remain for you in spite of the difficulties in your life.

Talk

1. If you feel comfortable, talk about a time when you did something really stupid. What impact did it leave on you?
2. Talk about a time when you experienced mercy from someone even though you should have been punished. How did it feel?
3. How do you think God is like a mother?
4. Who is someone in your life who has shown you the unconditional love of God?

Act

Stretch yourself to think about God as a mother. Think about God's motherly compassion, nurture, and unconditional love and reflect on how you can also extend this to other people. Reflect on everything in your life as gift. Each breath, each conversation, each moment is pure grace. Ask God to help you be more present and "accept your acceptance" (a quote from Paul Tillich).

Pray

Our Mother in heaven, thank you for your compassion. Thank you for gathering us together like a mother hen gathers her chicks. Remind us of your promise to comfort us in spite of the mistakes that we have made. Remind us that your loving spirit will never stop hovering over the waters of chaos in our lives. Amen.

Write/Draw

"Catch Me" by AGAPE*
Featured on *Sprinkle Sunshine*

Extra extra read all about it
My single mother struggled while them other mothers doubted
Hurt by guys. No surprise.
Internalized my momma's tears in my momma's eyes.
I'm thankful grateful even when it was painful
You came to the rain and you painted a rainbow.
You were there to hear my borning cry.
You gave life to me and put grace in the morning sky.
Ran once and you still forgive me.
Ran 2 times and you still forgive me.
Ran three times and you still were with me.
Thought your mercy cup was empty but it spills so quickly.
I feel so empty when I do dirt.
But you're Sofia. You're pneuma and you're also Mother Earth.
When I chirp you chirp back compassion's song.
When I come back home you leave the lights on.

CHORUS:
Accept me catch me bless me just don't forget me. (That's right) (3x)
Leave the lights on cause I might come home tonight.

He was sick of the mess so he bounced out the nest.
Cloudy vision wild living and his daddy's "Express".
He would chill in the club. He was living it up.
Spending dividends on women in Dominican pub.
This hustling gangsta with this struggle and anger
When it came to the 'caine homie wasn't a stranger.
Gang bang with bangers served rocks on the block.
Licked shots with the glock when the block was hot.
Rock bottom got 'em. Summer changed to autumn.
Once the feds caught 'em it really was a problem
Cold out no doubt must go home now.
But if his father sees him then he'll probably get thrown out.
Wondered what his pops would say he was just a block away.
Stopped to pray poppa came heard him say, "be not afraid."
Old man ran at him with a big old hug.
Told his brothers, "put ya love into this big ole thug."
You were found to the lost then lost to the found.
Till the day you came back I was holding it down.
Kill the calf grab your kicks and get ya robe on.
Invite your older brother cause the beat goes on.

The beat goes on the beat goes on....
Invite your little sister cause the beat goes on.
The beat goes on the beat goes on...
Invite your enemies cause the beat goes on.
The beat goes on the beat goes on......

Chapter 4

Stephanie
The Joy of AGAPE*

Rejoice in the Lord always. Again I will say, Rejoice. Let your gentleness be known to everyone. The Lord is near. Do not worry about anything, but in everything by prayer and supplication with thanksgiving let your requests be made known to God. Philippians 4:4–6

What is it with the religious end zone celebrations in the NFL? Vikings wide receiver Cris Carter used to point up to the sky to give his savior a "shout out" after each miraculous catch. After pulverizing the opposing quarterback with a violent hit, Steelers safety Troy Palamolou used to cross himself. And, unless you were under a rock for the last few years you know about "The Tebow." As amusing as it is to watch this "pumped up piety," I can't help but wonder, have these Christian players read Philippians 4:4–9? Paul says to "Rejoice *always*" (v. 4). So, where is Troy's religious cross motion when *he* is the one who has been knocked on his butt by an opponent? It doesn't seem to happen.

What if these NFL players followed Paul's advice to the Philippians? I can see it now: QB Russell Wilson's sternum would nearly break in two as he is sacked. While he is lying there, he would point up to the sky to thank God that he still has most of his limbs in tact. Or how about a coach, who has just lost a Super Bowl by thirty points, saying something afterward like, "I just want to give God all the glory," as the media would sit there in disbelief? Our world has no idea what to do with faith-filled "losers."

Imagine if a young person came home from a game and the first question his parents asked was, "Hey son. How was the game? Did you put yourself into each play, compete graciously, enjoy each healthy moment, and develop more camaraderie with your teammates while appreciating the privilege and opportunity to play organized sports while many kids your age can't play because of various tragic reasons?"

And our faith communities reflect this too (i.e. "How many people worship at your church?"). Most Christian best sellers talk so much about "winning" that you would think they were written by Charlie Sheen.

Paul's day was no different. There were "name it and claim it" movements bubbling up in both the Jewish and imperial Roman temples of worship, just like they are in our churches, synagogues, and mosques today. Back in the day, if you had money and "success," the default belief was that it was because you were more faithful than others. If you were struggling financially, were sick or disabled, were unable to have children, and so forth, many believed that it was because of a weakness in your faith, and God was somehow punishing you. Hopefully most of us have met enough poor, sick saints and enough rich, buff jerks to know that this mechanical connection between worldly "success" and faith is complete BS.

We cannot avoid suffering in this life. It is unfortunately a part of the deal. Jesus tells us in Matthew 5:45 that God "sends rain on the righteous and the unrighteous." But, we still can't resist the urge to think that if we just send enough praise up to God that blessings will start to come down. Is this really supposed to be why we praise God? So we can get stuff?! God is not a cosmic barista (i.e. "I'll take a 'grande'-sized mansion with a full shot of health and wealth. Go easy on the suffering").

When we read Paul's words "Rejoice in the Lord always" (Philippians 4:4), we think to ourselves: ALWAYS? Really Paul? That's easy for you to say. You were probably writing this from your mansion while counting your money, squeezing your hot spouse, and hugging your beautiful kids like many of the other popular ministers of today. Anyone can say that in that situation . . . wait . . . what's that you say, Paul? You don't have a partner or any kids? What about the mansion, though? You don't have that either? In fact, come to find out, you were experiencing persecution and writing many of these letters **from jail** ? *(Insert Homer Simpson doh! in here.)*

And then as we are staggering from the impact of this radical phrase, Paul smacks us with another shocking spiritual uppercut: "*Again*, I will say, 'rejoice'"! This is Paul's shocking "mic drop" moment as he walks off the stage. Paul is not saying that if we just think about puppies and rainbows all the time that life will be easy. Paul is saying life will be difficult but we can still find reasons to give thanks to the One who is with us through all of it. Rejoicing is different than being happy all the time. It is more an orientation of one's life than a description of one's mood.

Paul's idea of still having joy, even during difficult times, was a foreign concept to me until I met a girl in a wheelchair named Stephanie. "I can't lift my arms very well to shake your hand. You'll have to settle for a shoulder," she joked before she launched into her life story. "I've been in this 'chariot' since birth because I am a queen." She started rattling off dozens of her medical diagnoses like a fourth-year med student. "I get to spend a lot of time in hospitals. I go there for the good food," she cracked. Then she asked me (only it didn't really feel like a question): "You're going to let me dance on stage with you, right?"

"Of course!" I said nervously, having no idea how she was going to "dance" given her physical limitations.

We wheeled her on to the stage as the music played. Stephanie wasn't moving. I wondered if I had made a mistake. I didn't want to embarrass her in front of so many people. And then . . . she started warming up. Stephanie began to playfully twirl her chair with her remote control back and forth, around and around. Suddenly she began to beam with a smile that was too big for her face. She looked up to heaven and closed her eyes slowly. She reverently placed both of her hands over her heart. Then, as quickly as she pulled them in, she somehow mustered the strength to raise both of her arms up to the sky. She opened up her hands and poured them out, as if to say, "I give everything I have to you." All of us tearfully took in her "joyful arm offering" to God and gave her a standing ovation.

She came backstage after the show and I asked her, "How do you do it, Stephanie? How do you keep such a positive attitude?" She said to me, "Dave, when you've had as many brushes with death as I have, it makes you very thankful for life." Paraphrasing Eckhart Tolle, there are two ways to be joyful: The first way is to get what you want. The second way is to *not* get what you want.

Somehow Stephanie was thanking God even in her own "losses." Her joy wasn't a campy bubbliness that was naïve to struggle, but it was a deep sense that God was with her regardless of how difficult her circumstances were. Since my encounter with Stephanie I have tried to celebrate each breath as a gift. My epiphany wasn't from watching football players dance in the end zone—it was from watching a frail, dying girl twirl in a wheelchair. Shalom.

Think

There are two ways to be joyful: The first is to get what you want, and the second is to *not* get what you want. Think about the "positive" and "negative" experiences in your life over the last few years. First Thessalonians 5:18 says, "Give thanks in all circumstances." Is there still a potential for joy in response to some of your difficult circumstances?

Talk

1. How do you think our praise *to* God and our blessings *from* God are connected?
2. Matthew 5:45 says, God "sends rains on the righteous and the unrighteous." What do you think this means?
3. Do you think it is realistic to give thanks in all circumstances? Explain.
4. What do competition and faith have to do with each other?

Act

Make a gratitude list and thank God for fifty blessings in your life ("God, thanks for breath, thanks for a roof, thanks for food, thanks for medicine, thanks for clothes, thanks for healthy limbs . . ."). Try to get as miniscule as possible ("God, thanks for molecules of air that keep me alive, thanks for the microbodies that fight off sickness . . .").

Pray

God, thank you for the blessings in our life that we appreciate in the moment and the ones that we don't. Amen.

Write/Draw

"Rejoice" by AGAPE*
Featured on *Sprinkle Sunshine*

CHORUS:
Creation sings your praise. This is a day that God has made. Rejoice! Rejoice! And again I say rejoice (2x)

You help the mother eagle fly.
Made the stars that's in the sky.
Gave the ocean all its life.
This is why we sing.

(CHORUS)

Agape Rap:
Rejoicing with every rhyme
Rejoicing like all the time.
Crib where I live that's a roof on my head.
Clothes in the closet and shoes under the bed.
Got a Beautiful wife and a beautiful life
not because I'm good or I'm doing it right.
But just because the universe is filled with abundance,
signs of the blessings and the miracles and wonders.
Ever since the beginning my sins are forgiven
I rinse in the river slight glimpse of the heaven sky.
In fact in tact wonder where my sins at?
Blessed me from my Twins hat down to where my timbs at.
Let me sing and just rush the stage.
Everything with breath must give praise.
Re jo I to the C E Everyone with rejoice w/me.

(CHORUS)

Every time we see a majestic sun set.
Heart flex in the chest we're blessed with one breath.
Rejoice! Rejoice! And again I say Rejoice!
Every time that we find humankind on the grind
open up their mind and let ya love shine.
Rejoice! Rejoice! And again I say Rejoice!

We will rock. Got it locked. We'll give you all that we got.
We'll spread your love to everyone we see on every block (2x)

BRIDGE:
Let us give thanks in all circumstances (4x)

(CHORUS)

From the rising up of the sun to the going down of the same
Rejoicing again Rejoicing again. Rejoicing again and again and again.

Glory to glory to glory to glory to glory

Every knee every tongue every heart everyone.
Universal praise has already begun

Throw your voices up. Throw your praises up.
Give thanks to Creator till your days are up (4x)
When I say "re re" you say "joice" Re re...joice re re...joice
When I say "re" you say "joice' re "joice" rejoice everybody rejoice!

Chapter 5

Hatija
The Healing of AGAPE*

Out of the depths I cry to you, O Lord. Lord, hear my voice! Let your ears be attentive to the voice of my supplications! If you, O Lord, should mark iniquities, Lord, who could stand? But there is forgiveness with you, so that you may be revered. I wait for the Lord, my soul waits, and in his word I hope; my soul waits for the Lord more than those who watch for the morning, more than those who watch for the morning. Psalm 130:1–6

As our plane landed in Bosnia we saw dozens of "Caution: Land Mines" signs that were scattered along the runway. The heavily armed European Union troops greeted us with cold stares. Standing by the baggage claim was an elderly man with a large scar across his face. We were not in Kansas anymore (unless Kansas was a place with land mines and scary dudes holding machine guns). We were a group of affluent young people in a war-torn country trying to teach peace-making to traumatized kids. I thought this was a good idea when I first signed up but now I wasn't so sure. Was it too much to ask to not want to get blown up by a land mine? Was I being irrational that I preferred my guards to have normal sized guns? This seemed like a reasonable request. I also could have really used a Starbucks. I shouldn't have been surprised that overpriced coffee hadn't yet made its way to a war-torn country with burnt-out buildings and 40 percent unemployment but a guy can hope.

We were suddenly "hug tackled" by five joyful Bosnian teenagers. "Welcome Americans!" shouted a smiley, brunette woman in her twenties. "My name is Amina. We are sooo glad you are here. Whoot! Whoot!" she chirped in her adorable Bosnian accent. Her joy was borderline campy. I had only seen that disposition from people who *hadn't* experienced heart-wrenching trauma before. Knowing what her country had been through I could tell that she had earned every ounce of optimism that she could muster. She had me at "Whoot! Whoot!"

As we rode on the bus, I asked Amina about the polka dot buildings that we saw throughout the city. "Those are not polka dots, Dave," she said to me politely. "Those are holes from mortar shells."

She pointed out other "sights" throughout the city: "Those are the buildings I used to hide behind to avoid the snipers on my way to school." "This is the bridge that we would walk under to avoid gunfire." "The red paint on the sidewalk is to cover up the grenade holes."

She went on and on with trauma after trauma. Had all of this really happened in our own lifetime? How could a city go from the Olympic games to war games in such a short amount of time? Deep down I think some of us stubbornly refused to believe her in hopes that we could retain our hope in humanity . . . and our sanity.

The second day we were there we arrived in a town called Srebrenica. A woman named Hatija approached our bus the moment we stopped. Before any of us could even say "hi" she had already launched into her heartbreaking life story:

It was a Thursday. I remember it like it was yesterday. I called my husband at work and they said he was not there. I thought that was very strange. I called my brother to see if he had heard from him, but he wasn't there either. I called my papa because he is my protector and he *always* answers his phone. But he didn't answer. That's when I knew something was wrong. I was counting the seconds as I waited for my son to come home. I wanted to give him a big hug and have peace of mind knowing that he was okay. Fifteen years later and I am still waiting for him to come home.

She showed us a picture of a young man with broad shoulders and a big smile. "My son is handsome, isn't he?" she asked, as tears cascaded down her face. "He was an innocent boy. He deserved to live!"

In July of 1995 more than eight thousand men and boys were brutally murdered by a Serbian paramilitary unit in what is known as the "Srebrenica Massacre." In the span of twenty-four hours, Hatija lost her son, her husband, her father, and her brother to this horrific tragedy.

"After that sad day, I had to decide if I wanted to live or die," she said. "I decided to live."

Hatija formed an organization called "Mothers of Srebrenica."

Their aim was to help give hope to widows like her who have lost their husbands and sons in war. "I believe that every widow deserves justice," she explained to us. "I especially like to help Serbian women."

We assumed that it must have been an error in the translation when she said "*Serbian* women."

"Wait, don't you mean *Bosnian* women?" someone from our group asked, acknowledging that it had been Serbians that killed her entire family. "No, you heard me right. I like helping *Serbian* women," Hatija said.

"How can you possibly help Serbians after what they did to your family?" we asked her in disbelief.

"Because they are my neighbors and they are in need," she said nonchalantly. "When I help them I feel like I bring healing to my country and to my own heart as well." This Muslim woman embodied the good Samaritan story more than anybody I had ever met.

Hatija took us outside and showed us the memorial gravestones that rose up from the dying grass. Etched in black paint onto the white stone were thousands of names that seemed to go for miles. I traced a few of the names with my fingers and prayerfully whispered each of the names to myself: "Slobodon Millich, Petar Millich . . ." I began to look for the year they were born to try to figure out how old they were when they were killed. I came to a child who was born in 1989. This means that he was six years old when he died. I started to wonder about this boy: Did he have a big smile like my son? Did he like playing with trucks or kicking the soccer ball? All he was now was just a name on a rock. This seemed so unfair. I said a prayer for this child and for as many of the others as I could.

Hatija took me by the hand and walked with me slowly to show me a prayer that they had etched in one of the gravestones. "These are the words I live by," she said. "Please read them and remember them." I read the words slowly as she mouthed them along with me.

"In the name of God the most merciful, the most compassionate. We pray to Almighty God: May grievance become hope! May revenge become justice! And mothers' tears may become prayers that Srebrenica never happens again to no one anywhere. Amen!"

Hatija is the modern version of the story of Rizpah. In 2 Samuel we hear about Rizpah losing her son to senseless violence. She pleads for justice. She insists that King David give a proper burial for her child. She fights off the animals and stays with her son's corpse through the entire harvest until her wish is granted. Her family's dignity is restored, and her community is transformed through this one courageous act. Rizpah's grief became the fuel for her courage. Her tears became the water that nurtured her seeds of hope. Through God's Spirit, she overcame her struggle and found new life in it. You know: death and resurrection, that whole thing.

It's not *whether* we will feel sadness or despair in this life, but how we are able to cling to hope amidst the difficulty. It's in the scary darkness that Mary Magdalene ventures out and discovers the empty tomb (Mark 1:35). It's in the storm that Peter ventures out of the boat and encounters Jesus' saving hand (Matthew 14:29). It's in our despair where we find the need for hope, and it is in dying that we are brought to new life. I am so glad that I was able to witness God's Spirit at work in Bosnia. I saw more love in this war-torn land, more hope in this desperate place, and more Christ-like love in this Muslim country than I had ever seen in my life. Shalom.

Think

Think about some of the most evil things that humanity is capable of. Think of how God might be able to redeem it.

Talk

1. Why do you think human beings do such horrible things to each other? Do you think this will ever change?
2. Have you ever met a strong person who fought hard for love and justice? Have you ever been that person? Explain.
3. Describe a time when you saw Jesus even though you were not in a "Christian" setting.

Act

Think of one way to serve an "enemy" this week (i.e. shoveling the walk of a neighbor you disagree with politically). Go do it!

Pray

In the name of God the most merciful, the most compassionate. We pray to Almighty God: May grievance become hope! May revenge become justice! And mothers' tears may become prayers that Srebrenica never happens again to no one anywhere. Amen!

Write/Draw

"TEARS" by AGAPE*

Featured on *Paradoxology*

Close your eyes. Feel the wind.
Hear a voice deep within.
It's a woman that lost her whole family
Doesn't speak my language but she still can understand me
She told a story 'bout how she lost 'em
Buried in a mass grave couldn't find a coffin
Lost her son and her father on that very same day
Brother and her husband on that very same day
She heard the news pop
On her knees dropped thought she felt the earth stop on that very same day
Still so vivid she won't forget it
But she chose to live and forgive those that did it
I told her I was sorry for what had occurred
She looked at the gravestone and she read me these words and they said:

CHORUS:
Let our grievance turn to hope
And our darkness turn to light
Let our hatred turn to love
And our dying turn to life
When we feel despair
No that someone's there
Our tears will be our prayer

Let our tears be our prayer (2x)
When we cry lift us high
Let our tears be our prayer

Close your eyes. Feel the wind.
Hear a voice deep within
A girl 4 years old lies on the floor tries to ignore the cries
And the soldier's coldest eyes
She thought about how he looked as he took
The life of her whole family left her so shook
She thought about what she might say if she saw him some day
So she waited contemplated and she prayed
She had to look into those eyes
20 years later she can remember those eyes
Now she's flashing back never imagined that
She'd be looking again at those eyes
He froze. She froze. They froze

Her eyes stayed closed. Wonder what she chose?
She held out her hand she put it on his head
He fell to the floor crying this was what he said
Nothing…straight silence
Tears of baptism that washed away the violence
An invitation for transformation
And when the grace comes emancipation
She still has to see those eyes but they're no longer evil eyes
They tell a different story
Now she can see both sides
And when she hears the people's cries she gets to bring God glory.

(CHORUS)

Let my grieving lead into healing and hope
Let my weeping be for them a reason to cope
Let my sadness start to sow seed of strength
And let my tears be a prayer to whom I give thanks
Let the dark night be illuminated quickly
Source of the light walk with me
Hatred changed to grace in major ways
Gotta think long term doesn't come in 8 days
I pray with my tears and I plead with my sweat
That we won't forget the light even in the sunset
Whenever there's death there's always new breath of life
Tears water plants help them reach new heights
Teach you to fight for justice
When every piece of you would like some vengeance
But you can end this ill cycle that's there
Let my songs be my cry and let my tears be my prayer

(CHORUS)

Chapter 6

Do-Rag Saint
The Forgiveness of AGAPE*

When Jesus came to the place, he looked up and said to him, "Zacchaeus, hurry and come down; for I must stay at your house today." So he hurried down and was happy to welcome him. All who saw it began to grumble and said, "He has gone to be the guest of one who is a sinner." Zacchaeus stood there and said to the Lord, "Look, half of my possessions, Lord, I will give to the poor; and if I have defrauded anyone of anything, I will pay back four times as much." Then Jesus said to him, "Today salvation has come to this house, because he too is a son of Abraham. For the Son of Man came to seek out and to save the lost." Luke 19: 5–10

DO-
RAG
SAINT

James was a young man that you did not want to meet in a dark alley (or a well-lit alley, or, pretty much *any* alley for that matter). I have to admit, I was really bothered to see him walk into the sanctuary during the hip hop worship service at our church. Sure, we said, "all are welcome" on our sign but we didn't *really* mean it, especially with people like James. As he strutted slowly to his pew he started looking at each of the worshipers with his menacing stare. He wasn't supposed to be wearing headwear in the sanctuary but was I going to be the one to tell him to take his do-rag off? After all, his long white T-shirt was pushed out just enough by his midsection that I wasn't sure what he might be packing. I tried to ignore him but it's pretty hard to ignore a six foot four, 250 pound man wearing a shiny gold chain. As I asked people to stand up and dance, James just sat there with his tattooed-up arms folded. When I asked people to pray silently, James decided to laugh and joke with everyone around him.

While James looked at me with disdain, I told the worshipers about growing up without my father most of the time. "It was the forgiveness of my heavenly father that allowed me to forgive my earthly father," I told them. I doubted that anyone was hearing anything. James was commenting and laughing the entire time. I might have named myself after God's love but I was ready to pop him in the face.

As I was taking equipment down after the service, James began to walk over to me slowly. Was this going to have to be a let-me-take-my-rings-off kind of a confrontation? I was channeling every DMX video I had ever seen as the endorphins began to rush into my body. Who was I fooling? If we were going to fight I was in trouble. Luckily he had something else in mind. He mumbled, "I . . . heard . . . that little story you told about your dad and shit, is that shit . . . sorry, 'stuff' true?" He looked down as his voice trailed off. After a long awkward silence he looked directly in my eyes, his wandering pupils now settling into a desperate gaze. "I never knew my own dad." In between words, he would bow his head in silence. I waited patiently for him to say more.

"This dude keeps beating my mom, but she still stays with him." More silence. "My brother and I are involved in stuff that we don't want to be involved in." His body began to shake. "I've done some f'd up things, man." A few tears began to pour down his face. There was still no audible crying, just shaking and tears. "I feel like it's too late for God to do anything . . . I've run too far."

I whispered to him, "You can never run too far from God." And then he collapsed into my shoulder weeping. The cleansing tears cascaded down his face and onto my shirt. I kept repeating to him over and over again, "You can never run too far from God.
You can never run too far from God.
You can never run too far from God."

I prayed with him that God would give him the strength to accept the forgiveness that was already his. I prayed that God would show him a new way, free from violence and drugs. I also secretly prayed—*for me*—that God would forgive me for my judgments about James. It turns out we both needed to repent that day. He looked at me right in the face and said, "I am done with this street life shit. I'm getting out of the gang, and I'm getting rid of all my drugs. For real." He seemed sincere.

I believed him with all of my heart. After all, I have seen people who have had their lives totally turned upside down by God's grace. I want that to be true with James. I want this to be one of the stories about how everything worked out perfectly and how he is now a pastor who counsels gangbangers, but I can't honestly say that. James moved out of the neighborhood a few weeks after that, and I lost track of him. He might still be doing the same things as he was before for all I know. But I do know this, he was a beloved child of God before he walked in to our church that day, and he was a beloved child of God the moment he walked out. This hadn't changed. What had changed was my perception of James. And most importantly—James's perception of himself. It felt like two people were saved that day. James was "saved" of his shame, and I was "saved" of my self-righteous judgments.

In Luke 19:5 Jesus invites himself over for dinner at Zacchaeus's house. He does this in spite of the fact—or because of the fact—that Zacchaeus is a reviled tax collector (regarded as "highly" as today's drug dealers). "Who am I that Jesus would want to have a meal with me?" Zacchaeus must have thought. Jesus then tells Zacchaeus that he too "is a [child] of Abraham" (Luke 19:9). The thing is, Zacchaeus was *always* a child of Abraham. It's just that he (along with his tax-collector-hating neighbors) had forgotten it. The name *Zacchaeus* comes from the root word *zaccha,* which means "righteous one." Jesus' invitation doesn't change who Zacchaeus is at his core, but it radically redefines Zacchaeus's self-perception. This shift has the power to save. I think this is what Jesus was talking about when he says, "Today salvation has come to this house."

Salvation isn't necessarily about God changing us into somebody else. It's more about God awakening us to who we already are. Salvation is so much more than being rescued from a scary dude with a red face and horns. Salvation is about being saved from our own destructive monologue. Salvation is about being saved from the notion that we are all alone in this world. Salvation is about being saved from self-righteousness, and racism, and unhealthy addictions to things that don't bring life. This salvation is not something that we can do for ourselves. We try. But we keep screwing it up. We continually choose other things besides the way of God.

But the choice isn't ours. "You did not choose me, but I chose you" (John 15:16). The no-matter-what-ness of *agape* means that there is nothing we can do to make God love us any more or any less. This gift of salvation is permanent, and it extends to tax collectors, tatted-up drug dealers, and even judge-y rappers. No matter how far you or I may try to run, we can never run too far from God. Shalom.

Think

Think about the word *salvation* and what it means to you. Write the five most important words that come to mind.

Talk

1. Do you think there are sins that are too big for God to forgive? Explain.
2. Do you think "all" should be welcome in church? Are there any instances when you think "all are welcome" shouldn't apply in church?
3. Do you think it's realistic to forgive everyone regardless of what they have done to us? Explain.

Act

Think of five things that you need to be "saved" from. Lift each of them up to God in prayer and thank God that salvation is already yours.

Pray

Pray to God without speaking. Listen to God and repeat the word salvation at least ten times.

Write/Draw

"Somebody" by AGAPE*
Featured on *Sprinkle Sunshine*

My life is a mess trifling at best.
Walking these dogs at night with a vest.
I've been arrested about 10 times.
I've been shot at about 10 times.
In my prime, been in and out of crime.
Only got 9 lives and I don't wanna die.
Is there anybody listening? You don't how this been.
Drugs in my system and love's what I'm missin' and
quit drinking glycerin the game got me twisted and
all I need is just a hand life gotta switch it, man.
It's hard when you call the streets home.
My parents leave me alone.
I go home and they don't even be at home.
Slanging yay's what I don't condone.
But I only "Capone" cause my broken home
raised me this way pays me cause they never gave me a stable place to
play.
A place to stay and know that everything is cool.
14 years old done dropped out of school.
15 years old done copped me a gun.
16 years old was when I shot someone.
I never saw any love as a child.
I wanna love somebody but I don't know how.

CHORUS:
Somebody Somebody is shining on me (3x)
And Him is Jesus

I gotta man and I thought he was Mr. Right.
Turns out he was Mr. Not quite Right.
I got a night light every time we fight like tikes
I turn it on to try to keep the night bright.
In hind sight I should have seen it comin
when he stood there with that woman then I shoulda started running.
But I didn't though, and now he's hitting me like Riddick Bowe.
I shoulda quit it but I didn't so now I'm committed to this bitter road
and I'm feeling low.
Looking out my window praying.
It's been so painful the rainbows not quite here.
I think this whole thing needs to stop right here.
Bruise on my face when the dude's in the place

and it's moving to the basement.
Losin my patience.
Who's gonna make this all go away?
He'll kill me if I leave and it's hell if I stay.
Who's gonna love me with this baggage I'm packing?
Afraid that I'm lacking and I need to get it cracking.
Maybe it'll happen maybe there will be somebody to love me for me.

(CHORUS)
Ruyonga:
I'm standing at the church door staring at the downpour
and the lost souls everybody else looks down on.
Case in point exhibit A
this kid known to misbehave
cause he had his youth stripped from him in a twisted way.
Different day same garbage from a broken home.
Even with his parents there he felt he was on his own.
Seduced by the street suddenly he was holding chrome.
Took a life scene in jail thoughts of never going home.
Exhibit B where the b stands for battered wife
husband and abusive drunk he just wasn't acting right.
Meaning she got smacked around
the cycle is trapped her now
figured she deserve the pain she grew used to as a child.
But as a child of God those who don't or do behave.
Need to learn they are fearfully wonderfully made.
And every last one is welcome by the one above.
Giving what they need If all they need is someone to love.

Chapter 7

Papaya
The Reconciliation of AGAPE*

So out of the ground the Lord God formed every animal of the field and every bird of the air, and brought them to the man to see what he would call them; and whatever the man called every living creature, that was its name. Genesis 2:19

I usually drive the speed limit. At least I thought I did. So it seemed strange that an officer was pulling me over on my way home from a basketball game. I glanced down at my speedometer. It read "35." I looked up at the speed limit sign. It read "35." I glanced down at my seat belt. Check. I made sure my lights were on. Check. I looked in the backseat and saw my friends Terrance and Damien (who are both African American) shifting in their seats and getting very silent. Terrance started fumbling for his wallet. "Why was Terrance pulling out *his* ID?" I said to myself, "*I* was the one who was driving."

"Do you know why I pulled you over?" the officer asked me politely.

"No" I said naively.

"Your friends back there were flashing gang signs."

Terrance and Damien were both science nerds. There is a long list of things that they could have been doing. Goofy dancing? Maybe. Arrhythmic high-fives? Simulating chemistry equations with their "air pencils"? Probably. But, gang signs? Really? The officer's charges were totally bogus, and we all knew it. Pretty soon the officer was shining his flashlight in the backseat and asking my friends where they were going, if they had any drugs on them, and on and on. They answered each of his annoying questions with politeness and patience ("no sir, yes sir, no sir"). He asked for their IDs because he said he wanted to run them through his system ("Just to be safe," he explained to me). I had never seen human beings produce IDs so quickly in my life. Terrance and Damien both seemed like professional ID-puller-outers, like they had gone to school and trained for it or something.

As we were waiting for the officer to return, I became enraged. "This is freakin' ridiculous!" I shouted (only I'm pretty sure I didn't say, "freakin'"). "We have to find out this cop's badge number so we can report him. We are suing this dude! Who's with me?"

"You're a crazy white boy, Dave," Damien said while he chuckled.

"You actually think that's going to make a difference, don't you?" They smiled and shook their heads. The officer came back and gave us a warning. I kept asking myself, "Warning for what?" But that was the end of the story. Neither of my friends ever talked about it again. Watching the cop harass them like that was a top five traumatizing experience for me. Yet they seemed totally unfazed by it. Getting pulled over unjustly for them seemed like an annoying regular ritual. Like going to the dentist or renewing your license tabs. I wonder how we got to the place as humans where misjudging other sisters and brothers like this was acceptable. My theory is that we got to that place in the very beginning.

In the story of creation, God delighted in everything that God made and called it all "good."

When Adam took a stroll and saw all that God had created, he asked, "Yo, God, what is all this stuff?"

God answered him, "Adam, whatever you call it, that's what it is" (Scherer's Contemporary Revised Version). God basically gave Adam the power to label things how he saw fit. I can see Adam looking at this beautiful creation and saying, "Blessed, beloved, beautiful."

Then there was the whole papaya-eating incident. (Everyone says it was an "apple" but the Bible just says "fruit." Papaya is a fruit that tastes like barf to me so I have decided that it was definitely a papaya.) Humanity wanted to know the mind of God and be able to say who was "good" and who was "bad." After this, people started wearing "hater shades." Suddenly we began to label folks with value judgments about their appearance or personality, "ugly, fat, dumb." These became arbitrary ways to justify our mistreatment of each other (more from Scherer's version).

In the United States, color of skin is the reason we hate each other. In Bosnia people have the same color skin so they hate based on the name of the person. In Ireland they based it on the name of your street. In Rwanda they measured the sizes of people's noses to figure out which tribe they were from. We hate each other and fight wars because of street names and nose sizes? Really? Dang. Thanks a lot, Adam!

So, if we are all implicated in this racism thing, why do we pretend like everything is "all good"? If we are swimming in Adam's wake, then why do we act surprised when traces of racism are discovered in the water? If you are living in this world, you are "swimming in it" every day.

So what if the next time we found out that a celebrity was saying something ignorant, we took that time to examine our own ignorance that lives inside of us? What if the next time that a police officer is caught profiling, we used it as an opportunity for all of us to confess our own personal profiling moments? As angry as I was at that jerky officer when we were being pulled over, I have begun to realize: The same prejudice that lives in him also lives in me. I tried my best to swallow the "I'm not racist" pill, but this condition has to be treated daily. We all have to do this work.

If we had ended this horrible disease by now, we would not have white families in the United States worth thirteen times more than African American families (*FACT TANK*, Pew Research, Dec. 12, 2014). If we had left Adam's doo-doo behind then, we wouldn't have African Americans being sentenced for 59 percent of drug offenses in spite of being only 12 percent of the population of drug users ("Criminal Justice Fact Sheet," NAACP). Housing discrimination, unjust drug sentences, and the list of our systematic junk goes on and on. These forces of evil are like a horrible rash that just won't go away.

While 1 John talks about how "busted" we are all in this sinful system, it also says that if we confess it, God will forgive us and remove it from us. Part of this confession process is asking forgiveness from those we have wronged. Ironically, the only way that it can get better is by naming how crappy it is. Ask a doctor; it's hard to have a treatment plan without the diagnosis. Naming its ugliness is the only way that we can move forward. Luther named this process "Calling a thing what it is" (Heidelberg Disputation).

We don't go through this confession and reconciliation process to earn God's love. We don't do this to avoid feeling guilty. We don't even do it because it is the right thing to do. We do this because we genuinely need each other to be healthy and whole. Without the contribution of gifts from diverse peoples in our lives, we lose out on the fullness of God's kingdom. Without an appreciation of diversity, we miss the party that God is preparing for us. As my friend Yolanda likes to say, "If you don't like people that look different from you then you are going to hate heaven."

If Jesus is drawing all people unto him, then we need to start learning how to love all people so that we won't be miserable in a family with them. In the new world that God is creating, I imagine that Damien and Terrance won't have to produce IDs for the cop because he will already know this: Their identity is that they are beloved children of the most-high God! Shalom.

Think

Think of all of the moments of racism that you have had in the last month. Confess these to God and ask for forgiveness. Think of ways that you can ask and receive forgiveness from others whom you have hurt.

Talk

1. How do you think racism still shows up in our country? What about in our church?
2. How are faith and diversity related in your mind?
3. Do you think categorizing others is always a bad thing? Why or why not?
4. Do you think segregation or "self-selecting" will still happen in the new city that God is building? Why or why not?

Act

Spend fifteen minutes talking to someone whose experience is completely different than yours. Ask God to open your eyes to the fact that he or she is a beloved child of the most-high God.

Pray

God of all peoples, we confess to you that we have judged others for their outward appearance. We confess to you that we have participated in structures that are unjust. Forgive us for the racism we are aware of and for the racism we don't see. Remind us of the reality that we are all connected in your body. Help us to see others as brothers and sisters in your family. Amen.

Write/Draw

"Let's Face This" by AGAPE*
Featured on *Sprinkle Sunshine*

CHORUS:
Let's face this we're racist
We got judgment with no basis
We need love to replace this
Cause this hate is getting outrageous

Roll by the ghetto but ya never roll close at night
You'd rather keep a black man on your poster, right?
Watch the NBA to see what black folks is like.
The players are black and the coach is white.
Do you know what it's like with authenticity denied?
Won't say black trash but it's already implied.
Try to stop racism but it's already inside.
Remember those times that you'd call and he'd arrive.
And if he told you that he didn't kill him shorty lied.
If he asks for 40 acres better use a 45.
We're called to free our mind so we all can leave behind.
Problems we design so that all the people shine.
Please accept this apology of mine.
Justice is deaf and equality is blind.
This racist poet it takes one to know it.
Cause I'm not only racist I'm sexist and homophobic.

(CHORUS)

Krukid:
I was raised to hate y'all and why am I hating?
Don't blame me. Blame colonial-lie-zation.
Taught in schools y'all brought your rules and your bibles.
Hiding land treaties and nooses and rifles.
Separated families and enslaved my black peeps.
Made us villains "Black's evil", "black magic", "black sheep"
Littered black streets with cocaine to sell to each other
then returned to put us in jail cells with each other.
Back home shot us down for the uprisings
while chopping off little kids limbs off for diamonds.
Sent us to the back cause the front was whites only.
Even South African buses had "whites only".
"Whites good" "White sheet" "white collar" "white lie"
Whites did away with racism? Yeah, nice try.
Big city black choices: Rap, slang, or you ball.
And you wonder why I'm just as racist as you all.

Agape:
I'm not excited to ride in the plane with Mohammed
Oughta train thoughts to not get caught up those that follow Allah aren't
the same way as the terrorist embarrassed and ashamed.
Those Americans with arrogance I'm careful to claim.
I'm careless in the brain If I'm aware I can change.
I'm aware it's there but what about Sarah and Jane?
They bought his Che Gueverra chain they liked his hair and his name.
I'm not sure where I was trained.
It's not fair to blame Grandparents who were there to complain
about Mexican Americans who came to give their heritage a stain.
We're the same the game it aint fair.
Stop with the fake stare and telling 'em take care.
That's homeostasis that's quite dangerous.
Let's face this problem the human race is racist.

(CHORUS)

Sad that I'm racist this practice is ancient.
Masked all the hatred in the past when it came
and it crashed in my face and I asked to change it.
That's been amazing I'm actually changing. (2x)

Chapter 8

Nancy
The Presence of AGAPE*

How long, O Lord? Will you forget me forever?
How long will you hide your face from me?
How long must I bear pain in my soul,
and have sorrow in my heart all day long?
How long shall my enemy be exalted over me?
Consider and answer me, O Lord my God!
Give light to my eyes, or I will sleep of death,
and my enemy will say, "I have prevailed";
my foes will rejoice because I am shaken.
But I trusted in your steadfast love;
my heart shall rejoice in your salvation.
I will sing to the Lord,
because he has dealt bountifully with me. Psalm 13:1–6

It was a beautiful day at Bible camp. Bright sunshine. Blue sky. Swimming. Then the phone rang. Suddenly the dark clouds closed in. It turns out cancer's homing device had found another saint. My friend Nancy was a supermom for a son with Down syndrome and a mother to another dozen at-risk children. Nancy worked tirelessly on homeless prevention, community organizing, and eradicating poverty in the city of Minneapolis. Nancy threw around her smile like an Oprah giveaway ("you get a smile, you get a smile"). Nancy was a saint in the true sense of the word. Had Mother Teresa met Nancy there is a good chance that the saint from Calcutta might doubt whether she was doing enough good in the world. She was that amazing. So "why would this happen to *Nancy*?" Surely there was a crappy mom out there that could have gotten the disease. I had met plenty of them. Why not *one of them*? After all, the world was a better place with Nancy in it. God wanted the world to be a good place, right? So WTH?

When I finally had the chance to visit Nancy, I sat staring at a frail, bald woman reclined in stillness. Had I stopped at the wrong house? The Nancy I knew was fearless and strong. This Nancy looked like her spirit had already floated out of her body like in an old Tom and Jerry cartoon. Nancy opened her eyes slowly. Trying to mask my own shock, I greeted her with a forced smile. I was desperately searching for words that could make it all better. Bible verses? Inspirational quotes? Theological systems? They all felt like putting a bow tie on a turd. All I could figure out was that her cancer was just a big old turd, and that's all there was to it.

As we spoke, she would occasionally close her eyes and smile for extended periods of time. It was like she was seeing visions of a place beyond this world where crappy stuff like cancer doesn't exist. I longed to see whatever it was that was making her smile that big. Was she getting a preview of a world where death gets the smack down and life gets to wear the crown for once? Was she going back to her childhood and reflecting on happy memories from her life? I would have given anything to borrow God's View-Master and look at what she was seeing to make her smile. I firmly grasped her boney hand and prayed as hard as I knew how. I was hoping that if I held her hand tight enough, God would not be able to take her away from me. I gave her a hug and she whispered to me gently, "I'll miss you, Dave." I think I knew what she meant: My grip on her hand wasn't going to be nearly tight enough.

The next day I received a call from my friend Katy. She was trying to get a few words out between the loud sobs of those in the room with her. "Nancy . . . died . . . last . . . night . . . Dave." Collecting herself, she continued, "You were one of the last people to talk with her." And then she hung up. I sat in silence with the disconnected phone in my hand. It felt like Katy wasn't the only one who had hung up on me. I screamed at God for the next thirty minutes.

"How could you let this happen, God?" I yelled.

"I hate you right now!"

"Damn you!!"

I let God have it. Let's just say JC was not my BFF in this moment. "God, You're a coward, a punk, and a liar!"

"F-U!" I even screamed.

It was kind of therapeutic. I figured, if God *did* exist, God would be big enough to forgive me for my anger, and if God *didn't* exist it wouldn't matter anyway. I needed some sign that God hadn't left the building. Like Elvis, I started to wonder if God was on a desert island somewhere sipping piña coladas with Tupac and Jimmy Hoffa. God's vacation from my life felt like it had lasted the whole summer, and I was sick of it.

Brief disclaimer for the next part of the story: I tend to be a little wary when it comes to flash-bang miracle stories where people hear God's voice and it makes everything all better. I believe that faith is an incremental process and a winding journey, not a cheesy sitcom that wraps up neatly after thirty minutes. But, I actually think I heard God's voice in the middle of one of my WWF matches with my maker. I started hearing the phrase "I am with you." I know, four words, big deal. But it was something. There was also a feeling of peace that it carried with it. I kept waiting for the voice to say more. "I am with you," the voice said again. But there was nothing after that. Trust me I waited. I kept waiting for the voice to say, "I'm with you and you won't have to worry about any of your friends or family getting sick ever again." I kept waiting for the voice to say, "All of the problems of the world will go away instantly." Or "I will bring back Nancy from the dead like I did with Lazarus so you can hang out with her." But "I am with you" was all I got. Then, the moment faded just like that. Suddenly I was back to my life in the dorm room eating ramen noodles with my friends and watching "Spaceballs." I sometimes wonder if it really happened or if I just made the whole thing up in my mind. Those four words felt so clear at that time. It was only four words but, hey, that's more than some people ever get so I'll take it.

I have begun to realize the promise of God is presence, not perfection. The promise of God is to conquer death, not to eliminate it. It's not to completely take away the struggle and suffering, but to redeem it. Too often I hear about God's presence being like a Baywatch lifeguard. As if all we need to do is say the right words or recite the right prayer and Jesus will come running down the beach in his perfectly styled hair and red Speedo as he rescues us from the waves that are crashing down on us. Anyone who has been through a tragedy knows that is not exactly how it works (I'll give you a minute to get the Speedo image out of your mind). God is present whether we pray for God's presence or not. We don't need to pray for God's ability to show up for us. We need to pray for *our* ability to show up for God.

When I am ready to run away from my faith, I cling to scripture like Psalm 13. In this lament, the writer expresses how mad he is at God. "How long will you hide your face from me?" he asks God. The level of his pissed-off-ness gets muted when we read it on Sundays. We often sing the happy John Tesh-like section of the Psalms and avoid all of the dark Kurt Cobain-ish parts. But there are plenty of them. In this Psalm the writer is "keeping it real" in a Cobainian kind of way (with a little bit of Tesh-ness sprinkled in). Many people attribute this writing to David, one of the prominent heroes of our faith. The same David described as "a man after God's own heart." *That* David! Somehow in the midst of all of his desperation ("how long, O Lord, will you forget me forever?") he is able to muster up this statement, "But I trust in your steadfast love" (Psalm 13:5). How does he speak these words of hope just a few verses after his desperate cries and anger? Is he just trying to "land the plane" and make everything all better like the end of an episode of Full House? Did he have a miraculous flash-bang experience in the middle of writing his Psalm like I did? I don't know. Maybe David knew that he had to go directly through his anger to get to the joy that was waiting on the other side. Maybe David's willingness to be honest with God is not evidence of his doubt but actually his faith. I tend to only show my fears, doubts, and anger in front of those that I really trust. Maybe in a weird way my venting about Nancy was actually a sign of my *trust* that I have in God?

Jesus never promises an alleviation of our pain or an "end suffering" button on our cell phone that we can push. In fact, Jesus tells us that we *will* have trouble in this world (John 16:33). But, in the midst of our despair about this reality, he goes on to speak a word of promise, "Take courage; I have conquered the world!" This is the promise we have to cling to: the promise that God will pick up the broken pieces of this world and make something beautiful. The signs are there if we are looking for them.

A few days after Nancy's death we all packed into a huge downtown cathedral for her funeral. As I sat there in a cloud of sadness, I tried to keep my eyes open to look for God's light breaking through, just in case. I saw Nancy's daughter and son in the front pew hugging tightly and comforting each other. I saw our state senator give an eloquent speech about how we need to carry on Nancy's work of compassion for all people. I heard people from all walks of life singing songs of faith together beautifully. People held hands and prayed. People told jokes and laughed. We smiled. We sang. And we cried. We felt alive. We felt together. It was strangely beautiful. I think *this* must have been the vision that Nancy was seeing when she smiled and let go of my hand. Shalom.

Think

Think about all of the people who have come before you who have taught you about life and faith. Thank God for each one of them.

Talk

1. Why do you think people get cancer? What do you think God has to do with who gets cancer and who doesn't?
2. Psalm 13:1 says, "How long will you hide your face from me?" Have you ever had a period of time in your life where you felt like God was hiding from you? Explain.
3. Have you ever heard the voice of God? Describe when.
4. If God says that we still will have trouble in this world then why do we pray?

Act

Get in touch with your feelings about a situation that makes you sad/angry and express them fully in God's presence. Trust that God can hold all of it. With the same amount of passion that you express anger, look for signs that God is present in all of it.

Pray

God, thank you for those people who show us God's love and teach us about life. Thank you for your promise to stay with us in spite of our difficult circumstances. Give us courage to be real with you through the various stages of our lives. Amen.

Write/Draw

"God's There" by AGAPE*
Featured on *Many Rooms*

I got a tear puddle underneath the rubble of my trouble
But God is there with me through the struggle
You hold my hand while I clench my fist I'm pissed
When I say love everybody God I don't mean this
I wanna hurt somebody but I don't know where to start
The tears in my eyes can't put out the fire in my heart
so I cry to you god why did you god
take those people I feel violated God
but my feelings of anger shortly turn into sorrow
as I think what it will be like for a babies tomorrow
I can feel you right alongside me grieving
Our tears running down together on this sad evening
you hug me in a way that I've never felt
I feel light from the porches while the candles melt
I was dealt a bad hand but I know you still care
you're still working for my good I know you're still there

You were with me through the anger with me through the pain
with me as I saw the building going down in flames
you were with me as I cried with me as I wept
with me through the process there with me for every step
and has my heart still aching I'm just trying to get by
I can feel you wipe every tear from my eye
as I get scared wonder if the end is near
you say I'm your strength who shall you fear
As I get a little nervous and the times get hard
you say just be still and know that I'm God
as I'm shook wondering what's at the end of the page
you say I'm with you into the end of the age
I feel a little better but my heart is still hurting
I know you're there with me when the future's uncertain
down here and in the air Lord I feel you in the prayer
now I'm real aware of how you still are there

I pray for the rescue workers and the work that they do
may they find their rest in the strength in you
I pray for the families of the victims that were killed
May their tears turn to joy and may their hearts be healed
 pray for the leaders of this nation may they be wise
and think of ways instead of taking innocent lives
I pay for comfort I pray for unity I pray for peace

all the families and the people in the middle east
I pray for bin Laden and Saddam Hussein
may your grace watch over them just like rain
I pray for the US could be all be united?
working together one nation undivided
I pray for all the people growing up in this place
May they do your will and may they seek your face
I pray that you will is done everywhere
may we remember that we're loved and that you're there

Chapter 9

Bully Watcher
The Solidarity of AGAPE*

Pilate said to them, "Then what should I do with Jesus who is called the Messiah?" All of them said, "Let him be crucified!" Then he asked, "Why, what evil has he done?" But they shouted all the more, "Let him be crucified! Matthew 27:22

For a long time I claimed to be anti-bullying, but now I'm not so sure. I mean I don't give people wedgies in the hall or anything like that. I don't use slurs or pin people to their lockers while they beg to be left alone. My form of bullying is much more subtle. I guess it's more like "bully watching." It's that frozen feeling I get when I see someone being picked on, and I don't say anything. It's that paralysis I experience when I watch people get made fun of on TV, and I can't seem to turn the channel. Sometimes it's when my neighbor tells a gay joke, and I give a fake chuckle because I don't know what else to do. Or when I watch global injustices unfold on TV, and suddenly my butt feels like it's glued to the seat.

I have begun to realize that I am not the only "bully watcher" out there. There are a lot of us. There are dozens of popular shows on the air whose whole premise is to put down others for any number of reasons: being shallow, overweight, mentally ill, poorly dressed, singing off-key, and on and on. We can't seem to get enough of it. That's not the only form of bully watching. There are millions of us that witness hunger, human trafficking, and genocide on our TV screens while we sit on the couch and munch potato chips. And of course there is the unchallenged bullying that happens at schools. Why is that? Why are most of us opposed to bullying and yet so okay with bully watching?

I think it's because of three reasons (that all start with "D" because that's what you're supposed to do with this kind of stuff): Distance, Disbelief, and Dread.

1. Distance. As long as I perceive enough safe distance between the person who is being bullied and myself, I don't have to consider her or his feelings. It becomes easy to watch tragedy and disconnect from it when it is way "out there" somewhere. It gets much harder the closer it gets to home. We can watch the tabloids rip celebrities, but if I am Miley Cyrus's father things change dramatically. We can watch TV and see people die of hunger in the Sudan, but once we find out that a cousin is hungry our reaction is much different. In the body of Christ we actually *are* all cousins. When Jesus says that he is the vine and we are the branches, he is letting us know that we are all connected to each other whether we want to be or not. If one of us in our family suffers we all suffer together with him or her. How would we respond to bullying if we really believed that the person who was being bullied was our little brother, our sister, or our child?

2. Disbelief. Sometimes the bullying is right in front of our eyes, but we don't want to believe that it is actually happening. And even if we know that it is happening, we don't believe that there is anything that we can do to affect it. Our silence is what allows it to keep going. During Hitler's regime in Germany, there were many German citizens who just couldn't fathom that their neighbors were being systematically killed in such a cruel way. If they acknowledged that the genocide was happening, they would feel obligated to actually do something about it, which would be very inconvenient. So most of them sat frozen as it continued. There was at least one man, however, who refused to be a bully watcher. Dietrich Bonhoeffer was eventually hanged for his efforts to stand up to Hitler and the Nazis. He believed that being neutral wasn't an option. Not doing anything *was* doing something. He put it this way, "Silence in the face of evil is evil itself." Our efforts *do* matter, and they have the power to change the situation. As long as we buy the bullying magazines, click on the bullying websites, and watch the bullying TV shows, we allow the bullying to continue.

3. Dread. Let's not fool ourselves. Standing up to bullying is very scary. There are many legitimate reasons why we become so afraid of doing the right thing. I had a classmate in high school named Manny G. People made fun of Manny every day in science class for the whole year. I thought about standing up for him, but every time I was about to speak up, the thought crept into my mind, "What if they get mad at me and I lose my cool status?" "What if they turn on me and get violent?" Because of this fear I never said anything. Not once. Manny was tormented every day as I sat back and stayed silent. He needed to hear from me, and I let fear get the best of me. Martin Luther King Jr. once said, "It isn't the words of our enemies that we will remember, but the silence of our friends when we needed them the most." Manny needed me and I failed to stand up for him. I still carry shame with me to this day that I never spoke up and helped him. Many days I feel like the king of the bully watchers.

Unfortunately bully watching is not a new phenomenon. In the story of Jesus' crucifixion, there were many people who had the chance to stick up for him. His friend Peter had three chances to defend Jesus and he failed each time (he succumbed to Dread). Pontius Pilate had a chance to stand up and do the right thing but he also failed (he conveniently remained at a Distance). What about the soldiers that killed him? They could have spoken up for him (they were in Disbelief that they could do anything to change the situation). You figure the crowd would do something to stop it, right? Pilate gave them a chance to speak up if they thought that he was crucifying the wrong man. The crowd shouted, "Crucify him." Really? Not one person spoke up? How sad is that?

I always tell myself that I would have stuck up for Jesus if I were in that crowd. But is that actually true? If I couldn't stick up for Manny, what makes me think that I could stick up for Jesus? I am implicated in this story along with everyone else in that crowd. As I hear Jesus crying from the cross I am forced to remember all of the times I have been silent in the face of bullying. We are all guilty of bully watching at some point in our lives.

Caught up in the shame of my own "fallen-shortness," the only thing that gives me hope are the words that Jesus spoke as he was being crucified: "Father, forgive them; for they do not know what they are doing" (Luke 23:34). I believe that when he spoke those words, he was forgiving all of us. He was forgiving the soldiers that were driving the nails into his hands. He was forgiving Pontius Pilate for being a coward. He was forgiving the bloodthirsty crowd. He was forgiving his good friend Peter who had turned his back on him. And he was forgiving all of the bullies and bully watchers for all eternity. This includes you and me. By allowing his solidarity with humanity to go all the way to the cross, Jesus became the bullied. The most powerful willingly became powerless for the sake of others. Our God knows what it means to be vulnerable and stand with others. We don't do this work alone.

Despite Moses' "dread," he took courage and stood up to Pharaoh knowing that God was with him. Despite the socioeconomic "distance" between them, Ruth courageously stood in solidarity with Naomi like she was her own sister. Despite others' "disbelief" that she could stand up to King Xerxes's power, Esther stood up to Haman and Xerxes and saved millions of her people in the process. We stand on the shoulders of these "bully-watcher overcomers" as we advocate for others in the name of God.

So, who needs to be stood up for in your life? Are there things in your school happening that you know are wrong? Are there injustices happening in your community that you haven't had the courage to speak out against? Who are the "Mannys" in your life that need you? Speak up. Let your voice be heard. Stop watching the bullies before it is too late. Stand up to them with courage. Speak love and compassion to them and remember that sometimes the "them" is "you." God is with you. God has your back. You were born for such a time as this! Shalom.

Think

Think about all of the ways that you have been silent in the face of bullying. Hear the words of Jesus saying to you, "Father, forgive them; for they do not know what they are doing."

Talk

1. What are the ways that you bully watch? At school? TV? Social media? What prevents you from standing up for others?
2. Describe a time when you stood up for someone who was being mistreated.
3. How can Jesus help you when you are trying to stand up for others?
4. Do you think we will ever live in a "bully-free" society? Why or why not?

Act

Find one person in the next week that needs an advocate and stand up for her or him. Ask God to give you courage, compassion, and strength as you do this. This could be online or in person.

Pray

Dear God, thank you for standing with us and for us. Help us to stand with and for others. Amen.

Write/Draw

"Car Crash" by AGAPE*
Featured on *Rise Up*

16 Fresh and clean
Dream on the silver screen
Magazines was the queen
Seems she's become a fiend
Blonde Hair Princess
Small town Midwest
Big City big chest
Kids wanna get fresh
She's got white on our nose like a lifeguard
She's a hype got a show and a nice car
Life's hard sites are on being a bright star
If it wasn't for addiction she could probably make it quite far
Fact is like the other actresses skipping practices
In the bathroom hitting crack it isn't happiness
Don't nobody care they left that hottie there
Passed out at the party in that chair she was probably scared
She's making cash she's fading fast
This fame is a flash it isn't made to last
Stoned friends throwing parties in a house made of glass
All her friends don't jump in cuz they're just waiting for the crash

CHORUS:
We wonder how long will the star last
Before they fall we're waiting for the car crash (repeat)

Stars they play the game
Ours is craving fame
We get joy in this
Being a Voyeurist
Fans pay for them exposed
Cameras making offensive shows
Jessica Simpson knows
Pain buys expensive clothes
First Whitney Fell Then Brittney fell
Living in hell prison cell on crack like the liberty bell
How it ends up throw our hands up
Grab our bowling ball then we set the pins up
Set em up watch em fall
Is it real? Not at all
Loving to watch their misery then we bounce like a Soccer ball (x4)
Sit back eating chips

Hoping to see them slip I won't even trip
I do it too
Guess I'm right there with you (Car crash)

(CHORUS)

Pilate asked the crowd what he should go do with that man
They said kill em crucify em put those nails in his hand
So they watched him suffer necks were rubber from the action
It gave em satisfaction pain it was the main attraction
His boys slept and left him there to die
And when they asked his boys about him their reply was
"I don't know that man", Peter said, "I don't that man"
He's not my friend let me tell you again I repeat, "I don't that man"
So the crowds cheering
The blood's pouring
He cried out.
They showed No love for him.
They stripped him naked and made fun then they and they began
To pick on him spit on him his friends they just ran
Their shouting yelling waving
"Murder him kill him maim him"
Meanwhile he looked up and he asked
"Could you please forgive them father they just like a car crash?"

(CHORUS)

Chapter 10

Biscuits
The Patience of AGAPE*

But he himself went a day's journey into the wilderness, and came and sat down under a solitary broom tree. He asked that he might die: "It is enough; now, O Lord, take away my life, for I am no better than my ancestors." Then he lay down under the broom tree and fell asleep. Suddenly an angel touched him and said to him, "Get up and eat." He looked, and there at his head was a cake baked on hot stones, and a jar of water. He ate and drank, and lay down again. The angel of the Lord came a second time, touched him, and said, "Get up and eat, otherwise the journey will be too much for you." He got up, and ate and drank; then he went in the strength of that food forty days and forty nights to Horeb the mount of God. 1 Kings 19:4–8

The biblical prophets are straight up Gs. They speak truth to power. They stand up to "The Man" with authority, and they run things "like a boss" . . . but they also have their days. As you read their stories more closely, you begin to see that they had doubts and struggles. In fact there were days when they literally threw their hands in the air and said, "I give up, God." I can relate.

A few years ago I sat in a church parking lot in rural Minnesota while I stared at my own blank face in my rearview mirror. I was supposed to go inside the sanctuary and perform for a youth group. I was supposed to sing God's praises and tell them that life is wonderful. But I couldn't motivate myself to get out of the car. I had grown sick and tired of the hypocrisy I was seeing from everyone in the church. I was sick of the inauthentic banter and fake smiles. I was sick of pretending to have "found God" even though I knew that I was still *finding* God (or God was still finding me). And most of all, I was sick of Domino's pizza (those who do youth ministry know what I'm talking about). I was ready to drive out of the parking lot and never come back again.

Suddenly a handsome man with a soul patch and baggy cargo shorts came running toward the car. "AGAPE*! God bless you brother!" he yelled at me in his southern twang. His joyful smile was annoying the crap out of me. I desperately wanted to tell him to "screw off" but I resisted. Plus, I'm a competitor. I wasn't going to be "out-joyed" by this guy. I fired back "so great to see you" while I clenched my teeth and forced a large, horseshoe-shaped smile out of my mouth. "Take that, overly happy Christian guy," I thought to myself. He was not going to be outdone. He said to me eagerly, "We have been praying for you and this event for the past year." He was so frickin' sincere. People say that stuff all the time, but I got the impression that he really *was* actually praying about it. That's the most annoying thing. Dang it! I decided that I was glad that he was praying. The truth was, I hadn't prayed to God in over a year. I hoped that he was putting in a good word for me. "How am I going to get out of this car?" I thought to myself. Suddenly a powerful source of inspiration took over: money. I realized that I wasn't going to get paid unless I went in there and put on a happy Christian face. I got out of the car and lugged my heavy bags across the sun-scorched pavement. Sweating profusely and mumbling non-churchy words to myself with each step, I greeted the sound man with some kind of Christian cliché that he appreciated. Ugh, it was going to be a long night.

A few minutes before the concert, a middle-aged woman with too much makeup approached me. I was attempting to fly through my polite Christian banter and send her on her way so I could get ready for the show. She was not satisfied with my routine. She leaned in with a whisper, "We drove here from three hours away. My son, Blake, is desperate for something positive. He loves to dance to your music. Is there any way you could have him come on stage with you? It would really mean a lot." The scene was too familiar to me: I remember being a seven-year-old with a single mom, trying to dance away my family's pain and make it all better. I remember my mom trying to persuade positive adult males to spend five minutes with her son in hopes that it might cushion the blow of an absent father. I would have given her son a "warm fuzzy" if I could but I was fresh out.

As I began performing my brain started wandering. *Hmm, I wonder how many pews there are in this sanctuary . . . I wonder what I should eat after the show . . . I wonder who shot Biggie. . . . Hey, that guy in the front row has a really big forehead . . .* I was there entirely for the paycheck. That was when I realized that I had joined the ranks of "professional Christians." These are people who get paid to profess certain beliefs and have no wiggle room to express their doubts, fears, or general annoyances. I was doing my best to pull the sacrificial lamb's wool over their eyes and hope that none of them carried a "doubt detector" in his or her back pocket.

I glanced over and saw Blake lip-synching every word to my song about faith, hope, and love. He sprinted up to the stage and started jumping, rolling, and twisting as hard as he could with a huge, proud smile on his face. For this moment, he seemed impervious to the difficult painful journey that might be ahead of him and his family. As he danced, I took a long, loving look at him. I was hoping that if I stared at him long enough that I could brand him with a seal of protection. Like maybe my eyes could transmit power to him and help him overcome the "father wound" that so many of us have experienced. I held him in my heart for those moments as much as I knew how to do. And then, I broke it down while we had an epic dance battle. We did the running man. We did the worm. And we laughed and laughed. I walked off the stage with fresh images of his joyful dancing still in my mind as I got to the sales table.

Blake's mom immediately came up to me and grabbed my arm. The tears began to stream down her face. "Thank you," she said, looking to make sure her son wasn't listening. "I haven't seen Blake smile like that since the divorce. Thank you! Thank you!" I felt a little embarrassed that she was thanking me so profusely. "Your music and dancing has brought joy into Blake's life again." I smiled and said thank you, deciding not to tell her that her son had done the same thing in my life. I guess I didn't want to sound creepy.

After being on the run from Ahab and Jezebel, the prophet Elijah came to a place called Beersheba and decided that he had had enough. "Take away my life!" he says. This is a part of Elijah's story that most of us don't hear. Stories about depressed suicidal prophets tend to get left out of most Sunday school teachings. As he is lying there, an angel of the Lord shows up with a cake of bread baked over hot coals and some water. My dad told me that we would understand this cake today as something like a biscuit.

You can imagine Elijah's disappointment. There he is, fresh off slaying prophets with a big old pyro show, and what does God bring him? Out comes a little salty, doughy, bite-sized hockey puck. Elijah takes the biscuit and the water, eats it and then immediately goes back to bed. Apparently he wasn't all that impressed. I can hear Elijah saying to himself, "I have just slain a thousand prophets and all I get is a biscuit? Wake me up when you have something better than that." The angel comes back a second time and touches him while he says "arise" (*qwum* in Hebrew). The second time is a charm. Elijah finally gets up and is fed by that small biscuit for forty days and forty nights. Dang, that must have been some kind of biscuit! Then he heads to the mountain called Horeb to wait for God. There was a big earthquake, wind, and fire, but God wasn't in any of it. God finally shows up to Elijah in a "sound of sheer silence" (1 Kings 19:12).

For those of us that are feeling worn out, it is easy to want the big mountaintop, earthquake experience. For those of us who feel hungry, it is easy to look for the large banquets rather than the small wafer that is already sitting in the palm of our hand. Sometimes we want the majestic voice from the mountains but instead all we get is a goofy, breakdancing kid who makes us smile.

God is calling us to arise from our sleep and bless the world with our gifts. There are others who feel like giving up. They need small reminders that they are not alone. You don't feel qualified? That's okay. God uses suicidal prophets, burnt-out rappers, and ordinary people to be God's messengers. You might not see the evidence right away, but as Teilhard de Chardin said, "Trust in the slow work of God." God doesn't just show up just through loud shouts and big banquets. God shows up through sheer silence and biscuits. Shalom.

Think

Think about how God has given you biscuits over the years. What are the small reminders right now that God is in your life and watching over you?

Talk

1. What frustrates you about your church? What would you change if you could?
2. Talk about a time when you received a biscuit (a small reminder of God's love for you).
3. Do you know people in your life who need a biscuit? How might you be able to encourage them with God's love?

Act

Your mission, should you choose to accept it, is to give one biscuit to someone who needs it today. If you are struggling right now, your other mission is to look for small signs that God is with you (silence and biscuits).

Pray

God, thank you for the biscuits that you give us each day. For those of us who are ready to give up, make yourself known so that we might continue your work. Give us eyes to see you in all of the small ways that you come to us. In your name we pray, Amen.

Write/Draw

"Biscuits" by AGAPE*
Featured on *Many Rooms*

Meet Kyle he's your average nice guy
Run of the mill pretty smart quite shy
This High Schooler's had enough he's about to give up
Expectations to them he couldn't live up
He had a plan to end it
Get out of dodge there was a gun in the garage
he thought he'd grab it and he'd bend it
Towards his head it didn't matter when he'd send it
On a platter didn't think he really had a friend it's sad
Cuz his dad wasn't there to prepare him for things
Like the wonder and the joy life brings
Ostracism was hard Kyle lost the vision was scarred
The man on the cross was with him is God
Skip that mess. No friends or a family so how am I blessed?
You know what I'm gon' do today when I get home from school today
I'm gonna grab the 22 and then I'm gonna shoot away
He stepped up got on the bus
Thinking Arthur to ashes and Ash to dust
Then he sat down a background of death was here
He heard a faint voice in his ear
"Can I sit here?"
He smiled when he talked
"We need to hang out and rock.
I heard about you they told me you're the new kid on the block"
Nobody had ever reached out to Kyle like that
Just a little conversation brought his smile right back
Instead of going home thinking his life was done
He realized his life had just begun
'Cuz Sometimes when you can't see God
All you can see are the angels from his squad (2x)
With biscuits 40 days and 40 nights
And everything is gonna be alright

CHORUS:
Gonna be alright (In the desert 40 days and 40 nights)

Elijah was a rider others tried to
Light up the fire but his would light up higher
Ahab had waited fabricated like a textile
"Grab this hated liar force him into exile"
Now on the run wanted to give up and drop it

He said, "I'm no better than my forefathers as a prophet"
Hungry in the desert, he started to cry
"Lord I do try but I must die.
I'm getting out the kitchen I can't take the heat"
Then he heard a voice, "Get up take this cake and eat"
A stranger was near an angel appeared and showed him
"You can do it!" a couple other things he told him
See God loved him but when he missed it
All that God gave him was an iddy biddy biscuit.
To feed on that 40 days and 40 nights
And everything is gonna be alright.

(CHORUS)

Chapter 11

Enough
The Grace of AGAPE*

Once when Jesus was praying alone, with only the disciples near him, he asked them, "Who do the crowds say that I am?" They answered, "John the Baptist; but others, Elijah; and still others, that one of the ancient prophets has arisen. He said to them, "But who do you say that I am?" Peter answered, "The Messiah of God." Luke 9:18–20

I have a friend named Jay. She is beautiful in a make-every-other-girl-mad-for-even-trying-kind of way. She has a great smile. She radiates light. She's pretty much the bomb. One day a group of us were going to watch a movie when Jay made a weird announcement: "I'm going to take my sweatshirt off and wear my tank top." We all watched as she put her hands on her zipper slowly to pull it down. And then she stopped. She put her hands back on the zipper, and then she stopped again. Finally she took a deep breath and took the zipper all the way down, removing her sweatshirt and revealing her arms to us. Flashing a nervous smile, Jay shuffled her feet back and forth as she uncovered her pale, emaciated body. We all gasped as we saw hundreds of bright red scars creeping from her shoulders down to her wrists like stripes on a candy cane. "I can't wait to watch this movie you guys," she said cutting through the awkward silence. My friends began whispering to me, "Go talk to her." What was I going to say? In fact, I had even made comments to Jay about my preference for skinny girls. I was a part of the problem, not the solution.

I reluctantly walked into the kitchen with Jay hoping that wise Spirit-led words would appear to me magically. This was an opportunity to transmit the gospel to a soul that was in need. This was a chance to provide the encouragement that was going to help her become healthy. My words of grace in the moment were: "What the hell is going on with you?" I couldn't stop staring at her arms. She finally looked down at the scars herself like she had never seen them. The fake smile had finally begun to wear off. "When I look in the mirror I don't see any beauty," she mumbled.

"My dad used to tell me that I needed to lose weight . . . I was never thin enough for him . . . I was never pretty enough for the kids in my school . . . I was never holy enough for the people at my church . . . It seems like no matter how hard I try, I am never enough for anyone." She sat there in my arms crying as I searched for the right words to speak. She wasn't the only one who was feeling inadequate in that moment.

In Luke 9:18 Jesus turns to his disciples and asks, "Who do the crowds say that I am?" I can't help but wonder why he's asking that question. Is he giving them a pop quiz? ("Okay, class, who is the son of man? Say it with me on the count of three: 1-2-3. JESUS!") Is he asking it in more of a rhetorical-Beyonce-say-my-name-say-my-name kind of way? It's possible. But my friend Ladd proposed another idea that has stuck with me: What if Jesus was having an identity crisis? Think about it for a minute: Christians believe that Jesus was fully human. Humans have questions like this all the time. He had been tempted in the wilderness, rejected by his hometown, and was developing a teenage-heartthrob-like following. These can all mess with a guy's sense of self. As his usual sources of identity are crumbling around him maybe he is legitimately looking for affirmation like the rest of us human beings do from time to time. Unfortunately "the crowd" was clueless about who he was. They had a long list of possible identities for him, none of which were accurate.

If we look to "the crowd" to determine our real identity, we are going to be sorely disappointed. They often tell us we are not skinny enough, not strong enough, not smart enough, not rich enough, not famous enough, not talented enough, not good enough parents, not good enough spouses, not good enough students, not good enough at our job, not good enough Christians, and more. The weight loss industry alone made over twenty *billion* dollars a few years ago (*"20/20 Online,* ABC News)! No wonder we have trouble hearing any other voices. The "not good enough" industry is a lucrative enterprise.

Looking back, my pep talk for Jay was pretty corny: "Say with me 'I am beautiful.'" She wasn't feeling it. Instead we sat in silence. Long. Awkward. Silence. I didn't know what else to do so I just prayed, "God, help Jay see herself the way that you see her." We sat there in more silence. Long. Awkward. Silence. After what felt like an eternity, I finally asked Jay, "Do you hear God saying anything to you?"

"Maybe," she said while seeming slightly annoyed and surprised at the same time.

"What do you think God is saying?"

"I think God might be saying, 'my grace is enough.'"

While I was secretly hoping that this would make it all better, Jay still has a long way to go. There are women in her treatment program who are more than sixty years old. They have struggled with anorexia and/or bulimia their whole lives. Those "not good enough" voices don't go away. In fact sometimes they get stronger and stronger.

In the baptism of Jesus, the Spirit descended in like a dove and said, "You are my Son, the Beloved; with you I am well pleased" (Luke 3:22). This was the same spirit that hovered over the waters of creation and the same spirit that hovered over the waters on the day that Jay was baptized. The crucial question to ask is not: "Who does the crowd say that I am?" but "Who does the Spirit say that I am?" If we listen carefully we will hear a still small voice pierce through all of the other voices. It says to us, "You are enough. My grace is enough. I have knitted you together in the womb. You are fearfully and wonder-fully made. I know the hairs on your head. I have claimed you. You don't need to lose another pound for me to love you. You don't need to accomplish anything more before I will love you. I love you simply because you are made in my image and you are mine."

There are many nights when I hold my sons in my arms before they go to bed. On these nights I think about all of the "not good enough" messages that they will receive from this world. I think about all of the ways that I have reinforced this message with my less-than perfect parenting. And then I look at their beautiful faces, and mark-ing them with the cross on their foreheads, I say to them similar words that Jay heard when that water was splashed on her head, "'You are a beloved child of God, sealed in the waters of the Holy Spirit, and marked with the cross of Christ forever.' Your mommy, your daddy, and God all love you and there's nothing you can do about it." Shalom.

Think
Think about all of the competing "not good enough voices in your head" about who you are. Now hear these words from Psalm 139: "I am fearfully and wonderfully made" (v. 14).

Talk
1. What are the ways that you compare yourself to others?
2. Who are the people in your life who tell you that you are not enough?
3. Do you know people who struggle with cutting and/or an eating disorder? How do you show up to support them?
4. What are the signs from God that remind you that you are "enough"?

Act
Look in front of the mirror and repeat these words ten times: "I am enough. God's grace is enough." Do this ten times.

Pray
God, you know the hairs on our head. You knitted us together and formed us in the womb. You call us each by name. We belong to you. Help us see ourselves the way that you see us. Let your voice speak louder than all of the other voices in our head that tell us that we are not good enough. Open our ears to hear your words, "my grace is sufficient." Amen.

Write/Draw

"Beautiful" by AGAPE*
Featured on *Enough*

Hey 'ma, why you soaked in tears?
You broke the mirrors of hope which awoke the fears
Of not being good enough
Not being cute enough.
Not being thin enough.
Not seeing in the cup.
That it's half full. You only see the half empty.
Thanks to MTV we see that simply.
Not by what they do say, it's what they don't say.
Not the songs they will play it's ones they won't play.
Constant images of women that I've never seen before.
Unhealthiness breeds more.
But see, you're more than a body you are more than a smile.
You're a queen. You're a goddess. You are God's beloved child.
It's not for what you look like. It's what's in your heart, right?
If you can sing this song right then everything is alright.
It looks like you need a friend. Quit being unruly shaking your bootie for men.
And just look to the beauty within.

CHORUS:
Look inside to the beauty within. It's deeper than skin.
It's creepin' but you keeping it in (keeping it in) (2x)

Have you seen yourself? I'm looking for you. If you find you, let me know.
Your old self wastes away slow.
I can't recognize you in this hospital bed.
But I still got love for you. You got to know that.
I remember how it started last June in the classroom.
You'd eat a snack then it's back to the bathroom.
Showing what you aint got. Bones are showing in your tank top.
You think you're healthy, but they think not.
There was a funny sound of the money down the drain.
You're skinny now. Weigh a hundred twenty pounds
Now you're down to 95. 90's where you're trying to strive.
I feel like you might get to that kinda goal and finally die.
Why did I tell you that I only like girls that are thin.
I feel so guilty. Now my life is turning in.
But I always liked you 'cause you were my friend.
You're beautiful and it's deeper than skin.

(CHORUS)

Now I can't even tell what's normal anymore.
Can't tell the difference between a girl that's 14 and 24.
14 year olds wanna look mature.
While 24 year olds wanna look skinny for sure.
The taste of man reflects it.
You gain some weight he plans to exit.
So now you're anorexic.
It's like a cycle and we need to stop it
The media the t.v. gotta heed the topic.
Let's talk to each other about needing self-image.
We don't need more women in these eating health clinics.
Empower the feminine in men and then the gentlemen will shine through.
Let's treat you right when we find you.
You're perfect just the way you are I'm glad I found you
So much beauty that's within and around you.
Let it out shout, "I am beautiful"
Without a doubt you will know.

Chapter 12

Star Power
The Justice of AGAPE*

Therefore because you trample on the poor and take from them levies of grain, you have built houses of hewn stone, but you shall not live in them; you have planted pleasant vineyards, but you shall not drink their wine. . . . I hate, I despise your festivals, and I take no delight in your solemn assemblies. Even though you offer me your burnt offerings and grain offerings, I will not accept them; and the offerings of well-being of your fatted animals I will not look upon. Take away from me the noise of your songs; I will not listen to the melody of your harps. But let justice roll down like waters, and righteousness like an ever-flowing stream. Amos 5:11, 21–24

"God gets angry." Those three words from "turn or burn" preachers have made me shudder throughout my life. I want God to be happy with everyone all the time. I want my God's commands to be like the boss from *Office Space* ("Yeah, I'm gonna have to ask you to honor the Sabbath. Sorry about that. And, did you get the memo about not killing people? Could you go ahead and not do that for me? Thanks.")

Then I read a text like Amos 5:21: "I hate, I despise your festivals, and I take no delight in your solemn assemblies." I think to myself, "Dang God! That's kind of harsh isn't it? Lighten up." I hear about Jesus turning over tables and making a whip to drive the people out of the temple, and I'm like, "Dude, you are in charge of the whole universe. Don't be such a spazz!" And it's not just that God gets kind of peeved. God occasionally gets unhinged like a jealous lover on one of those basketball wives shows. It was easy for me to read about this behavior and begin to wonder if God might be a bit of a psychopath. But then I got a chance to go to Haiti.

We drove through Port au Prince past the thousands of makeshift tents that were set up for people displaced by the earthquake. As we got to one of the rural areas we saw dozens of kids carrying yellow industrial-sized buckets in their little hands. Being the ignorant American I asked our translator, "How long does it usually take for them to get water."

"Six hours," he replied.

"So when do they go to school?" I asked.

The translator was silent. Finally he said, "The families must decide whether they are going to put buckets in their child's hands or whether they are going to put books. They can't do both."

Anger began to pierce through my body. Clean water or education should not have to be a choice. As a father, I couldn't imagine having to make a decision like this for my sons. This was not fair. "What the heck are you doing about this?" I kept asking God in my mind. The more I was ranting against God, the more the rants started to feel directed toward my fellow Americans. "Why aren't *they* doing more about this?" I thought. And then, finally my rage was turned inward. It was as if God was turning the question back at me, "What are *you* doing about this?"

The more I think about it, the more relieved I am about the idea that God gets angry. Could you imagine a God who is totally indifferent to the suffering in Haiti? Imagine a God who just sits back and says, "One billion people lack access to clean water in this world (World Health Organization). No biggie." Or what about a God who feels no sadness about the fact that seventeen thousand ("U.N. Chief: Hunger Kills," CNN) kids will die today in our world from hunger and preventable causes? This God truly *would* be a psychopath.

The good news is that God loves us so much that God gets mad when all of us are not being cared for. God fights for each one of us fiercely like a mother cub because we all matter to God. Thank goodness!

In Psalm 3:7 the author says, "Rise up, O Lord!" Did he think that God was sleeping on the job a little bit and needed a pep talk? Or is this also a pep talk for himself? People ask me, "Is it *God* that rises up and brings justice or is it *us*?" My answer is always "yes." We do it together. God and us. Us and God. We are bound together in this project of healing the planet. St. Teresa of Avila puts it this way, "Christ has no body but ours." For some reason, God has chosen to accomplish God's enterprise of peace and justice through less than perfect humans like you and me.

Why would God choose *us* to do this work? Hasn't God seen our body of work before? Does God know something we don't?

Remember that game Super Mario Bros.? Normally Mario was just a short, little, chubby plumber with a bad mustache and goofy overalls. But then he would get this little star thingy. That star gave him a bunch of power and all of a sudden he could run and jump and save the princess. Before his crucifixion Jesus gives each of his screw-up disciples the equivalent of the Mario star. Through this star power of the Holy Spirit he tells them that they will do "greater things than these" (John 14:12). And guess what? They do. They heal people. They feed people. And they spread God's message throughout the world.

The anger I experienced in Haiti kept haunting me. Anger is not what sustains us, but it can sure get us off our butts sometimes. Through the power of the Spirit, I ended up planning a tour that raised money and awareness for water issues around the world. It wasn't perfect. But it was something. This could not have happened were it dependent on my power alone. Those who know me, know that spiritually I am the equivalent of a short, chubby plumber with a bad mustache and goofy overalls. But with the power of God's star thingy . . .

Some people handed me $2,500 checks and said, "Go build a well" (the average cost to bring clean water to a community in West Africa). Many people told me that they were inspired to do something similar in their own community. This justice stuff is doable because we aren't doing it alone. When we rise up, we rise up together with God.

So take that star power from the Spirit and defeat the unjust Bowser-like powers in your community. Let your righteous anger wake you up, but don't let anger consume you. Let God's compassion lead you to do something beautiful. Amos chapter 5 ends not in anger but with a pronouncement of God's new world that God is building through all of us: "Let justice roll down like waters, and righteousness like an ever-flowing stream" (v. 24). Shalom.

Think

Think about an injustice that makes you really mad. Imagine God holding you in your anger and encouraging you to do something about it.

Talk

1. What is an injustice in your school that makes you really mad? What about your community? The world?
2. Do you agree with the statement "God gets angry"? Why or why not.
3. Have you ever accomplished something that you didn't think was possible because of the power that you experienced through the Holy Spirit?
4. How might God be calling you to do something about an injustice that bothers you?

Act

Think of one thing that makes you mad in your community. Commit yourself to do one small thing to change it. For example, if hunger makes you mad, how can you use your gifts to bring awareness to hunger?

Pray

Dear God, thank you for the sense of justice that you place in each of our hearts. Ignite us with your passion to fight injustice in our communities and in the world. Fill us with your Spirit so that we can bring healing to the world and spread your love to people who need it. In your name we pray, Amen.

Write/Draw

"Rise Up Together" by AGAPE*

Featured on *Enough*

Building bridges breaking chains
Bearing burdens hope remains
We will rise up like the sun
Led by the risen one

CHORUS:
Rise up, O, God
With blessings on your people
Rise up together
Your love's gonna break the chains

This is the way that we rise Jesus will make us alive
Loving our neighbors and we love them in the name of our God
Compassion not just words but action
Rising from the ashes just like Lazarus from the casket
God is in the neighborhood
Get it? Get it? Got it? Good!
We got this assignment
No stopping keep shining
No you no me just us
Let's rise up together let's rise up

(CHORUS)

He is risen (forgiven redeemed)
He is risen (prisoners freed)
He is risen (risen is he)
He is risen (risen indeed)
So if we rise like he rose then we'll rise too
Though we're crying dying doesn't have the final
Neither does destruction,
We keeping on believing in that Jesus resurrection
We practice it, and get after it like mathematicians master it
It's happened the gavel of compassion God has been dropping it
All rise for the call
Healing for the nations and justice for us all
The hungry get to eat again worried find their peace within
Everybody's gonna get a home
and never have to wonder where they're gonna ever get to sleep again
JESUS blessed to bless fresh to death
Seeking peace more and more seeking war less and less

Resurrect these dry brittle bones that need it
Death has been defeated watch him rise up like a phoenix

(CHORUS)

Freedom from unjust oppression
Shelter for those with no home
Peace for those who live with violence
Love for those who feel alone

Welcome for those "on the outside"
Hope for all those "down and out"
Healing for those who are struggling
The time to rise is now!

(CHORUS)

Want to see you rise up (repeat)
We're rising up together with the one whose love will reign forever

About the Author

GRADUATE of Luther Seminary

PERFORMER at National Youth Gatherings for ELCA, LCMS, UMC, and COC

FOUNDER of Hip Hop Outreach and JUMP Ministries

SPEAKER at National Youth Workers Convention

WINNER of the 2009 Tommy Award for youth ministry

PRESENTER at Interfaith Forum for Hunger at Duke University

FACILITATOR of Leadership Development Intensive Training

CHAIRMAN of Building Bridges Conference for Diversity

CO-LEADER of Fellowship of Christian Athletes

BOARD MEMBER of Lutheran World Relief

YOUTH DIRECTOR at Mt. Olivet Lutheran Church in Minneapolis, MN

ARTIST IN RESIDENCE at Ramsey Fine Arts School in Minneapolis, MN

TEACHER at Urban Academy in Minneapolis, MN

MENTOR at First Lutheran Church in St. Peter, MN

MEMBER of an award-winning peer education group

PRESIDENT of Multicultural Student Union

FATHER of Matthew and Thomas

HUSBAND of Carolyn

SON of Barbara and John

Write/Draw

Write/Draw

Write/Draw

Write/Draw

Write/Draw

Write/Draw

Write/Draw